… # modern
PUNCH NEEDLE

LEISURE ARTS, INC. • Maumelle, Arkansas

The most fun thing about punch needle is how very easy it is to learn the craft; once you master it, the possibilities are endless! You can draw and punch all the motifs you like, use all the yarns you love and play with textures and materials. This is what I discovered when I first explored this craft, and that is what I want to teach you here.

In this book, you'll find a quick overview of what you can do with just a punch needle, some yarns and a piece of fabric (and, of course, a bit of patience!). You'll start with simple projects, which will add an original touch to your walls. By the end of those 4 projects, you will be a master of the punch needle! Then you'll be ready to move on to more complex projects, for you, for your child and for your home: pillows, brooches, pouch, or even a pouf. You may even want to experiment and create your own projects with your new-found skills!

I hope that you enjoy this journey with me as you discover punch needle!

Bérénice Robert

I began my crafty journey a few years ago with weaving, on a weaving loom made by my boyfriend. Then I created Woolthatgirl. It was the perfect way to introduce some creativity into my everyday life as a French scientific journalist. But it didn't take me long to want to try a new craft, so I learned macramé. When I first heard about punch needle at the end of 2017, I had to try, I knew I had to give it a go. I purchased my first punch needle and very quickly became addicted!

Note of Thanks

I would like to thank:

- Leisure Arts, for their trust in me to make this book; especially Tona and Megan for your kindness and patience.
- All my family and friends for their support, and in particular, my mum, for her unconditional support and precious advice.
- My sister Caroline — what would I have done without your help and, above all, your jokes?
- Jessica, for your help and careful reading and re-reading.
- Sandrina, for your support.
- My cat Koko, for not eating my yarn balls and not scratching my creations.
- And last, but not least, Maxime, for your patience, your everyday support and because you accept that I fill our tiny Parisian apartment with yarn balls and fabric.

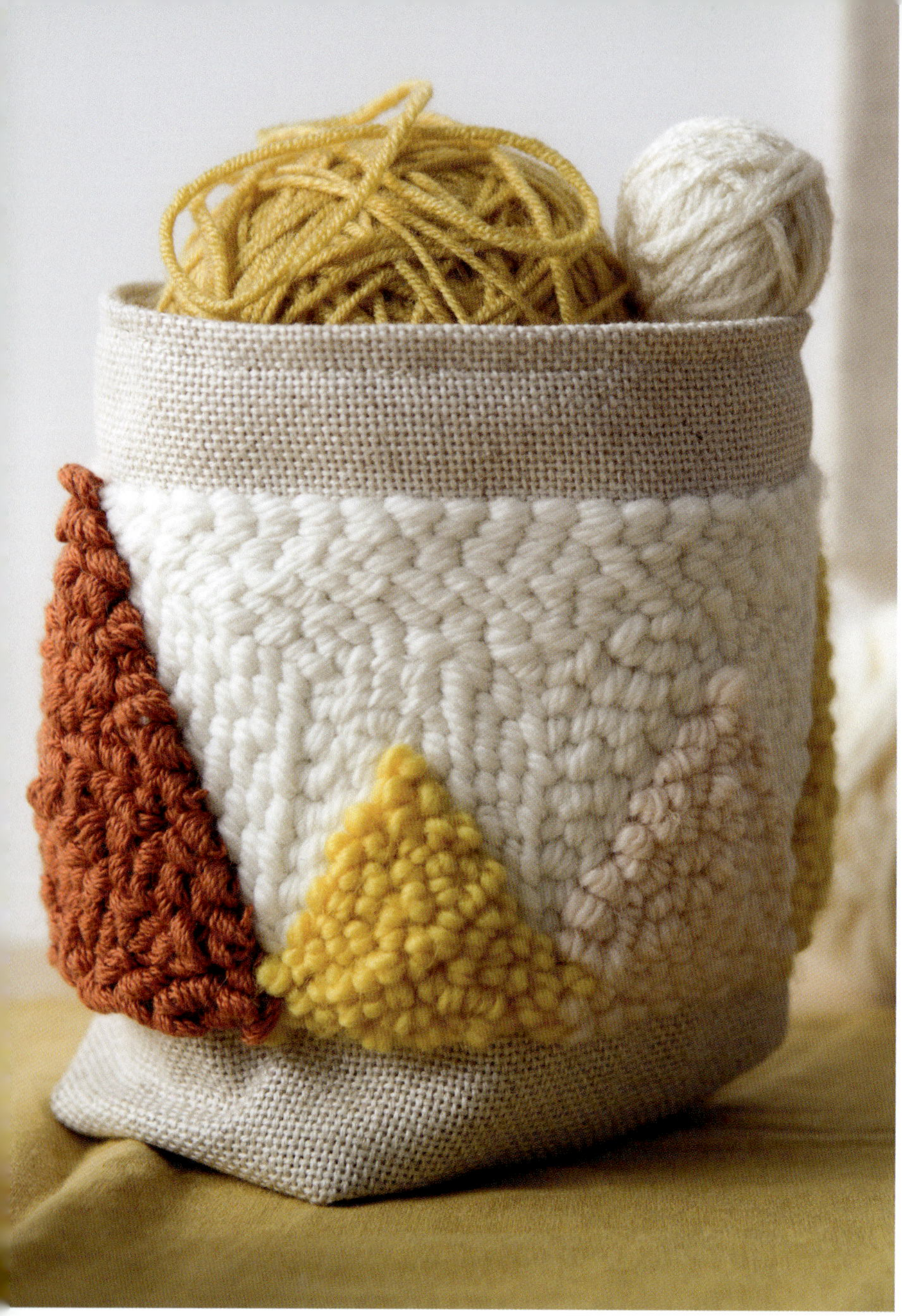
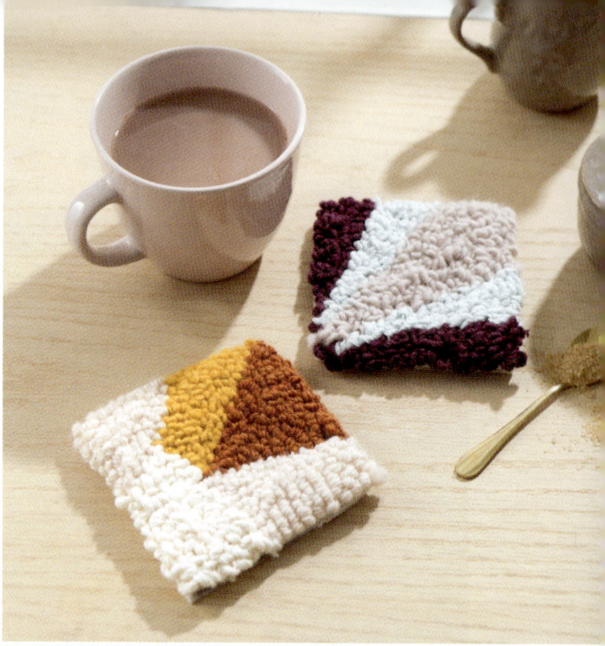
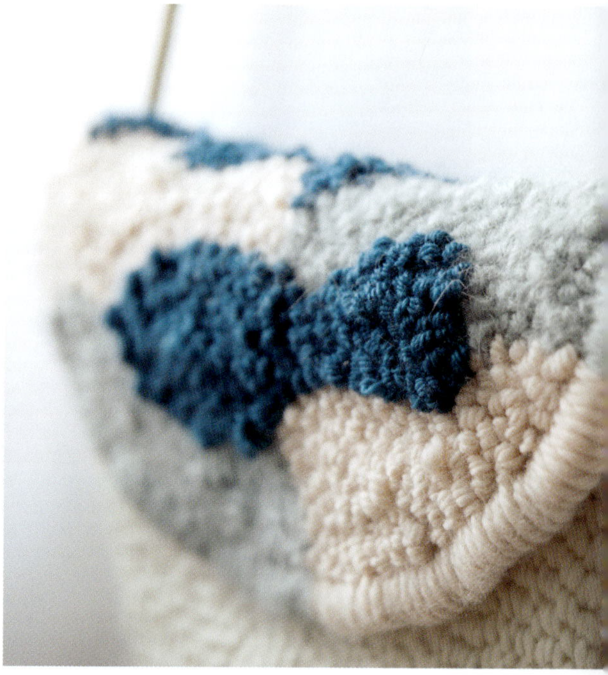
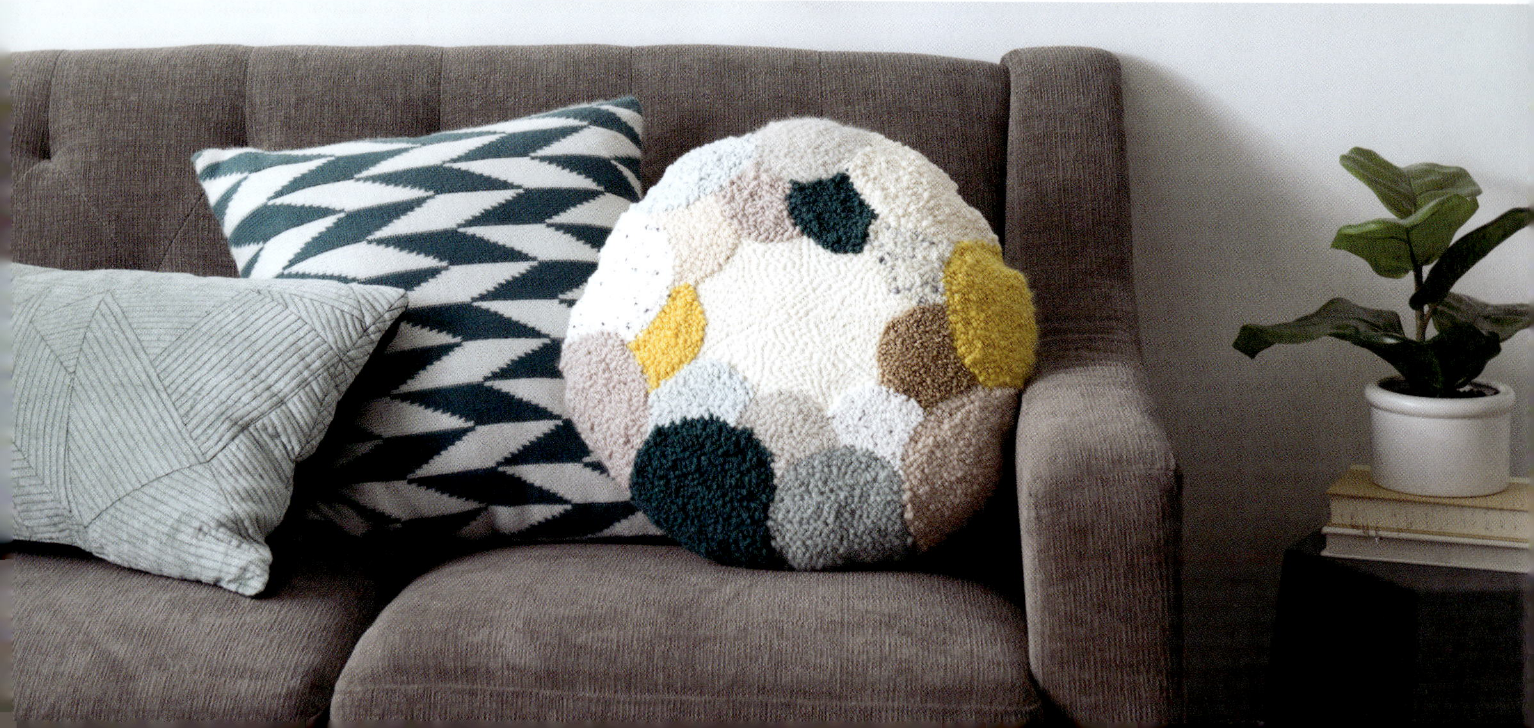

Contents

Bérénice Robert 4

Materials 6

How To Punch Needle 8

Hoop Wall Hanging 12

Abstract Landscape Frame 16

Fringed Wall Hanging 20

Arctic Fox Wall Hanging 24

Mermaid Pouch 28

Pin Trio 32

Floral Duo 36

Denim Jacket 40

Purse 44

Penguin Toy 48

Coaster Set 52

Rectangular Pillow 56

Storage Pouch 60

Round Pouf 64

Patterns 68

5

Materials

Hoops
A non-slip **hoop** is essential for holding the fabric drum-tight. Some hoops come with a stand or in sets of two with a stand; all types of hoops are available in many sizes.

Frames
A **frame** can also be used to hold the fabric for punching. Again, frames are available in many sizes.

Fabrics
A variety of **fabrics** can be used for punch needle. I like to use Floba and Monk's cloth (a cross stitch or Swedish weaving fabric). Floba is an evenweave cross stitch fabric that comes in 18 and 25 count sizes.

Punch Needles
Needles are available in several sizes, both length and diameter. The diameter of the needle determines what size (thickness) yarn you can use, while the length determines the length of the loop left on the fabric.

The **Oxford Punch Needle**: we will use the #8 regular, the #10 fine, #10 regular and the #14 mini. The #8 regular needle uses bulky weight size 5 yarn, the #10 regular also uses bulky weight yarn (size 5) (or two strands of size 4 medium weight yarn), and the #10 fine and the #14 mini use size 4 medium weight yarn.

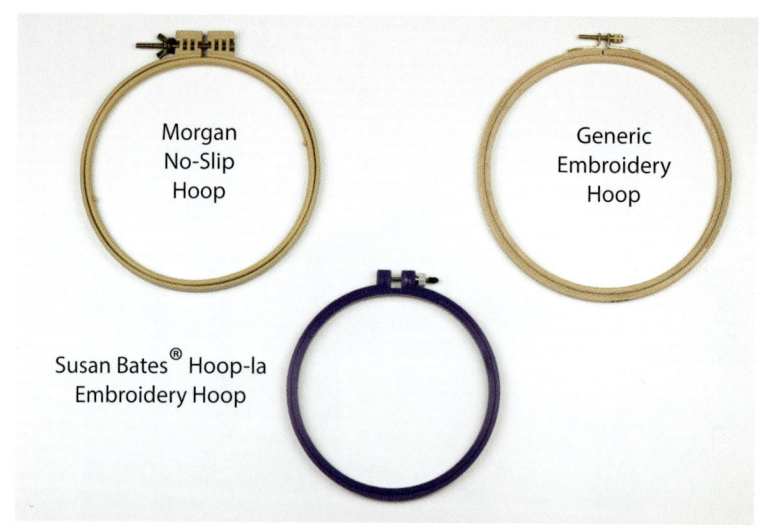

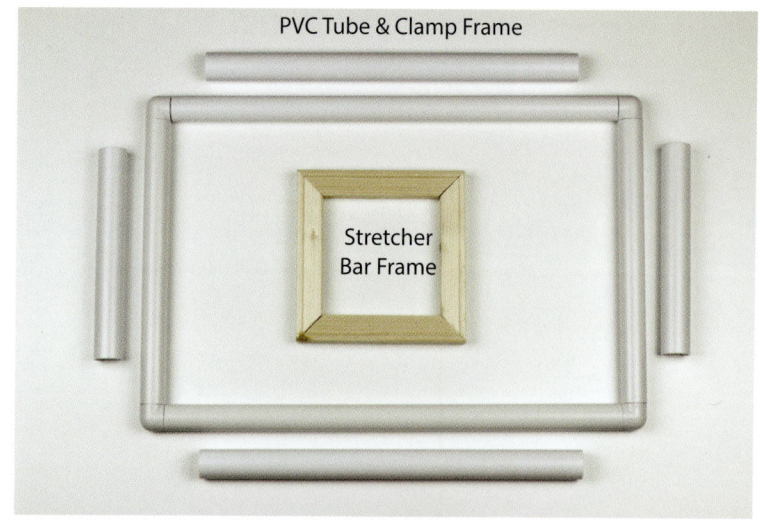

An **adjustable punch needle** can be used with size 5 yarn (or two strands of size 4 yarn). This needle has four needle positions, A, B, C and D, with A producing the longest loops and D producing the shortest loops. In position B, this needle can be used as a substitute for the Oxford punch needle #10 regular. One advantage to using this needle, you can choose the loop size.

Note: For the projects in this book that use the Oxford punch needle #10 regular, you can use position B on this adjustable punch needle.

The **Ultra-Punch® Needle** can be used with embroidery floss, lace weight (size 0) yarn or super fine (size 1 yarn). This needle is adjustable as well.

You may also need: a pencil to write on fabrics, size 18 tapestry needle, hand sewing needle, sewing thread, sewing machine, a staple gun, hot glue gun and glue sticks, embroidery scissors, sewing scissors and appliqué scissors.

Yarn

Yarn is available in many sizes. These projects use size 5 Bulky Weight yarn and size 4 Medium Weight yarn. The yarn skein has a symbol to show you the weight of that skein. You can use wool, acrylic, metallic, cotton, or any other yarn fiber combination to make these projects. Choose yarns that appeal to you and complement your style.

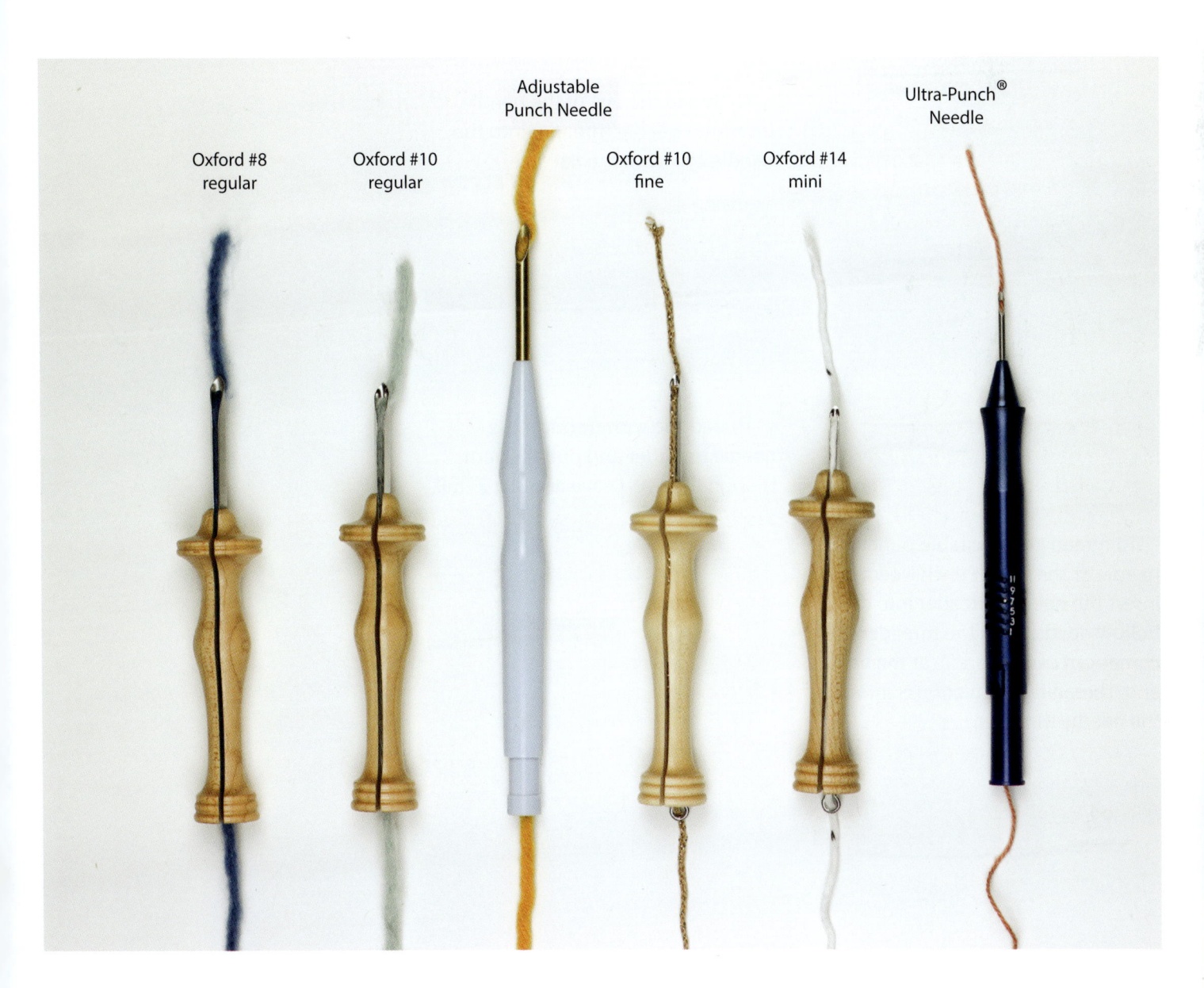

7

How to Punch Needle

Threading a Punch Needle Tool

To thread the Oxford Punch Needle, insert the yarn through the eye of the needle, starting from the side with the slot in the wood handle. Holding the yarn tail nearest the needle point, pull the yarn into the slot of the handle.

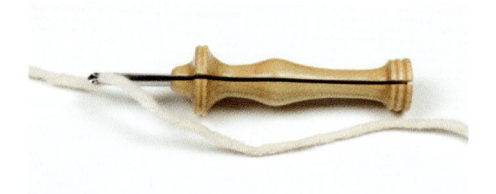

To thread an adjustable punch needle or the Ultra-Punch Needle, insert the needle threader into the hollow needle until the threader comes out of the handle at the other end. Thread the yarn or floss through the needle threader.

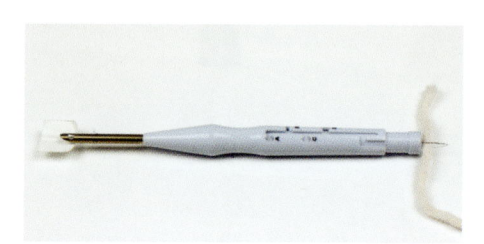

Pull the needle threader back out through the needle. Carefully pull the yarn or floss out of the needle threader.

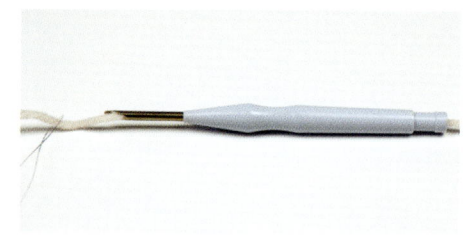

To thread the eye of the needle, insert the needle threader into the needle eye from the flat side.

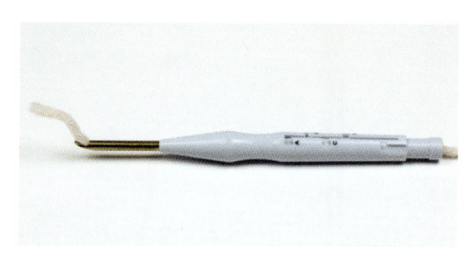

Thread the yarn through the needle threader and pull the yarn though the eye. Leave about a 2" tail.

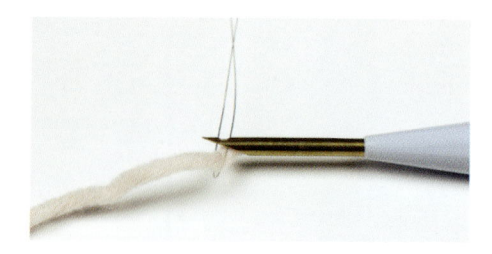

Placing the Fabric in the Hoop or Frame

To place fabric into a hoop, first separate the hoop rings. Place the smaller inner ring on a flat surface. Center the fabric over the inner ring. Place the larger outer ring over the inner ring. Tighten the screw, pulling the fabric taut as you tighten. It is important that the fabric be very taut (drum-tight) in the hoop.

To place fabric into a tube and clamp frame, first remove the clamps by sliding them off the PVC tubes. Place the tube frame on a flat surface. Center the fabric over the tube frame. Place 2 clamps over the fabric and snap them onto the tube frame. Place the remaining clamps over the fabric and snap onto the tube frame. Tighten the fabric by rotating the clamps outward from the center. It is important that the fabric be very taut (drum-tight) in the frame.

Transferring the Pattern

If the pattern is full size, trace the pattern onto tracing paper. If the pattern needs to be enlarged, photocopy the pattern as indicated, taping pieces together if necessary.

Tape the pattern to a sunny window or on a light box. Holding the hoop or frame up to the window, use a pencil to trace the design onto the fabric.

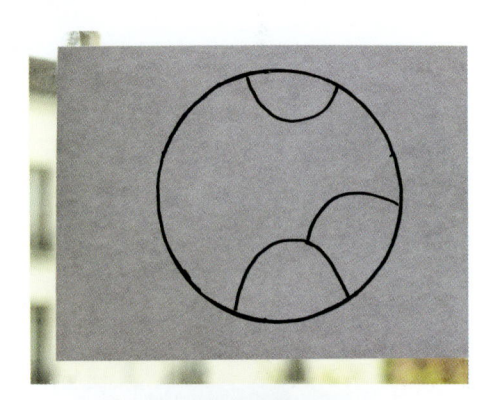

Using the Punch Needle Tool

Once your tool is threaded and the fabric is in a hoop or frame, you are ready to stitch. There are 3 types of stitches used in this book, Flat Stitches, Loop Stitches and Shag Stitches. Depending on the project, you may work on the front side of the design, the back side of the design or both. Flat Stitches are worked from the front side of the project, while Loop and Shag Stitches are worked from the back side.

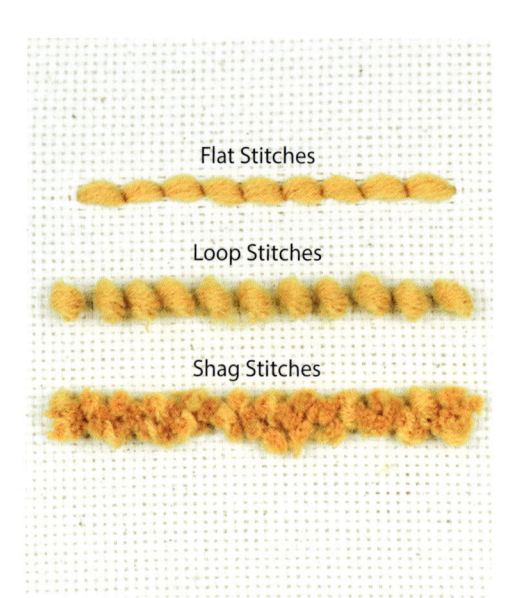

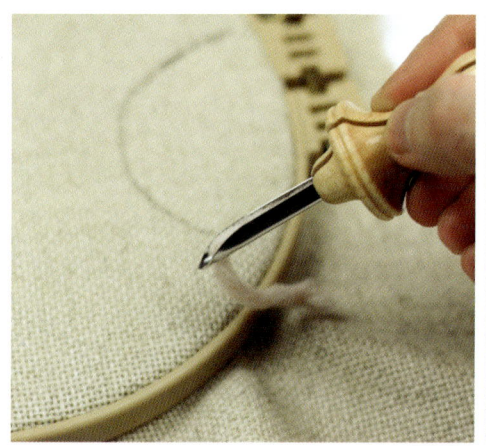

STITCHES

All 3 stitches are worked the same way. For the Flat Stitches, work from the **front** side of the design. Hold the tool like you would hold a pencil when writing. The angled or beveled edge should be on top and facing the direction you are going to punch.

I recommend you stitch the outline of the area you are punching and then fill the shape, working toward the middle and changing direction as desired to create texture. To make the first stitch, insert the needle into the fabric as far as it will go. Be sure to push the needle into the fabric as far as it will go every time you punch.

Now pull the needle out of the fabric, just pulling the needle barely out of the fabric. Slide the needle along the fabric surface and punch down into the fabric about $1/4$" away to make another stitch. Strive for a consistent stitch length. The stitch will be flat on the front side (the side you are looking at) and looped on the back side.

For the Loop Stitches, work from the **back** side of the design. Make the stitches the same as for Flat Stitches; the loops will be on the front side of the design.

Shag Stitches are Loop Stitches that are cut and lightly brushed.

TIPS

If you find that the stitch does not stay in the fabric, the yarn may have too much tension on it. Be sure the yarn is not getting caught on your hand, arm, sleeve or anything else.

If you are having trouble making a stitch or can only make one or two stitches at a time with the yarn, the yarn is most likely too thick. Try a thinner yarn.

Cutting the Yarn

When it is time to cut your yarn, leave the needle in the fabric toward the loop side of the work. Carefully turn the work over and clip the yarn even with the loops. Remove the needle.

Use the needle to push the original yarn tail to the loop side and trim it even with the loops.

If you will be using fusible interfacing on the back of your piece, carefully move the needle away from the stitches and trim the yarn close to the stitches.

Mixing Flat, Loop and Shag Stitches

Most of the projects in this book include a mix of Flat and Loop Stitches; a few have Shag Stitches thrown in as well. The pattern is only drawn on the front side of the fabric, so how do you know where to punch when working on the back side of the fabric? Easy; just mark the fabric by punching the area's outline.

Now remove the yarn and you have an outline of holes that you can follow to punch.

Hoop Wall Hanging

SHOPPING LIST

- Oxford Punch Needles: #14 mini, #10 fine and #10 regular

- 12" x 12" piece of 18 count Floba fabric

- 8" diameter embroidery hoop

- Size 5 Bulky Weight Yarn
  14 yards peach
  11 yards mustard
  6 yards grey-green

- Size 4 Medium Weight Yarn
  11 yards white/navy speckled cotton
  12 yards metallic gold

- Hot glue gun and glue sticks

13

1

2

3a

3b

4

14 www.leisurearts.com

Instructions

1. Place the fabric in the hoop, making sure it is drum-tight in the hoop.

2. Trim the fabric to about ¾" from the hoop.

3. Hot glue the cut fabric edges to the inner hoop. Once glue has cooled, you are ready to punch!

4. Transfer the pattern (page 68) to the fabric. It is not necessary to transfer the dashes and circles.

5. Referring to the table and photo, work the flat stitches from the front side of the fabric and the loop stitches from the back side of the fabric. After punching, trim all yarn ends.

Yarn	Needle	Stitch	Side of Fabric
Peach (P)	#10 regular	Flat	Front
Mustard (M)	#10 regular	Flat	Front
Grey-Green (GG)	#10 regular	Flat	Front
Metallic Gold (MG)	#14 mini	Flat	Front
White/Navy Speckled (WN)	#10 fine	Loop	Back

Abstract Landscape Frame

SHOPPING LIST

- Oxford Punch Needles: #10 regular, #10 fine and #8 regular

- 11" x 14" piece of 18 count Floba fabric

- 7" x 10" flat stretcher bar frame

- Size 5 Bulky Weight yarn
  8 yards peach
  13 yards rust
  8 yards mustard
  12 yards eggshell cotton

- Size 4 Medium Weight yarn
  12 yards metallic gold

- Appliqué scissors

- Staple gun

17

1a

Instructions

1. Place the fabric on the frame, stapling it to the frame back.

2. Transfer the pattern (page 70) to the fabric. It is not necessary to transfer the dashes and circles.

3. Referring to the table and photo, work the flat stitches from the front side of the fabric and the loop stitches from the back side of the fabric. Trim the eggshell loops with the appliqué scissors. Trim any yarn ends.

Yarn	Needle	Stitch	Side of Fabric
Peach (P)	#10 regular	Flat	Front
Rust (R)	#10 regular	Flat	Front
Mustard (M)	#10 regular	Loop	Back
Metallic Gold (MG)	#10 fine	Loop	Back
Eggshell (E)	#8 regular	Shag	Back

1b

2

3

19

Fringed Wall Hanging

SHOPPING LIST

- Oxford Punch Needle: #10 regular and #10 fine

- 16" x 16" piece of Monk's cloth fabric

- 12" diameter non-slip embroidery hoop

- 12" diameter embroidery hoop for display

- Size 18 tapestry needle

- Size 5 Bulky Weight yarn
  10 yards peach
  11 yards off-white
  11 yards mustard
  13 yards plum cotton
  55 yards eggshell cotton
     for fringe

- Size 4 Medium Weight yarn
  16 yards coral

- Scissors

- Hot glue and glue sticks

21

Instructions

1. Place the fabric in the hoop, making sure it is drum-tight in the hoop. Transfer the pattern (page 69) to the fabric. It is not necessary to transfer the dashes and circles.

2. For the fringe, cut 80 lengths of eggshell cotton yarn 24" each. Thread the tapestry needle with one length. Insert the needle into the fabric on the lowest drawn line; come out of the fabric 2 squares to the left from where you inserted the needle.

3. Pull the yarn through until the yarn is centered and the ends meet. Do not unthread the needle.

22 www.leisurearts.com

7

4. Insert the needle 4 squares to the right and come out of the fabric 2 squares to the left. Pull the yarn taut, locking the yarn into place. Repeat this process until you have added yarn fringe along the entire drawn line.

5. Add a second, staggered row of fringe using the same process.

6. Referring to the table and photo, work the flat stitches from the front side of the fabric and the loop stitches from the back side of the fabric. The area covered by the fringe stitches is not stitched.

7. Follow Steps 1-3, page 15, of *Hoop Wall Hanging* to place the fringed hanging in the display embroidery hoop. Trim the fringe as desired.

Yarn	Needle	Stitch	Side of Fabric
Peach (P)	#10 regular	Flat	Front
Off-White (OW)	#10 regular	Flat	Front
Mustard (M)	#10 regular	Loop	Back
Plum (PL)	#10 regular	Loop	Back
Coral (C)	#10 fine	Loop	Back

Arctic Fox Wall Hanging

SHOPPING LIST

- Oxford Punch Needle: #14 mini

- 12" x 12" piece of 18 count Floba fabric

- 8" diameter embroidery hoop

- Size 4 Medium Weight Yarn
  2 yards black
  12 yards off-white
  19 yards grey

- Hot glue gun and glue sticks

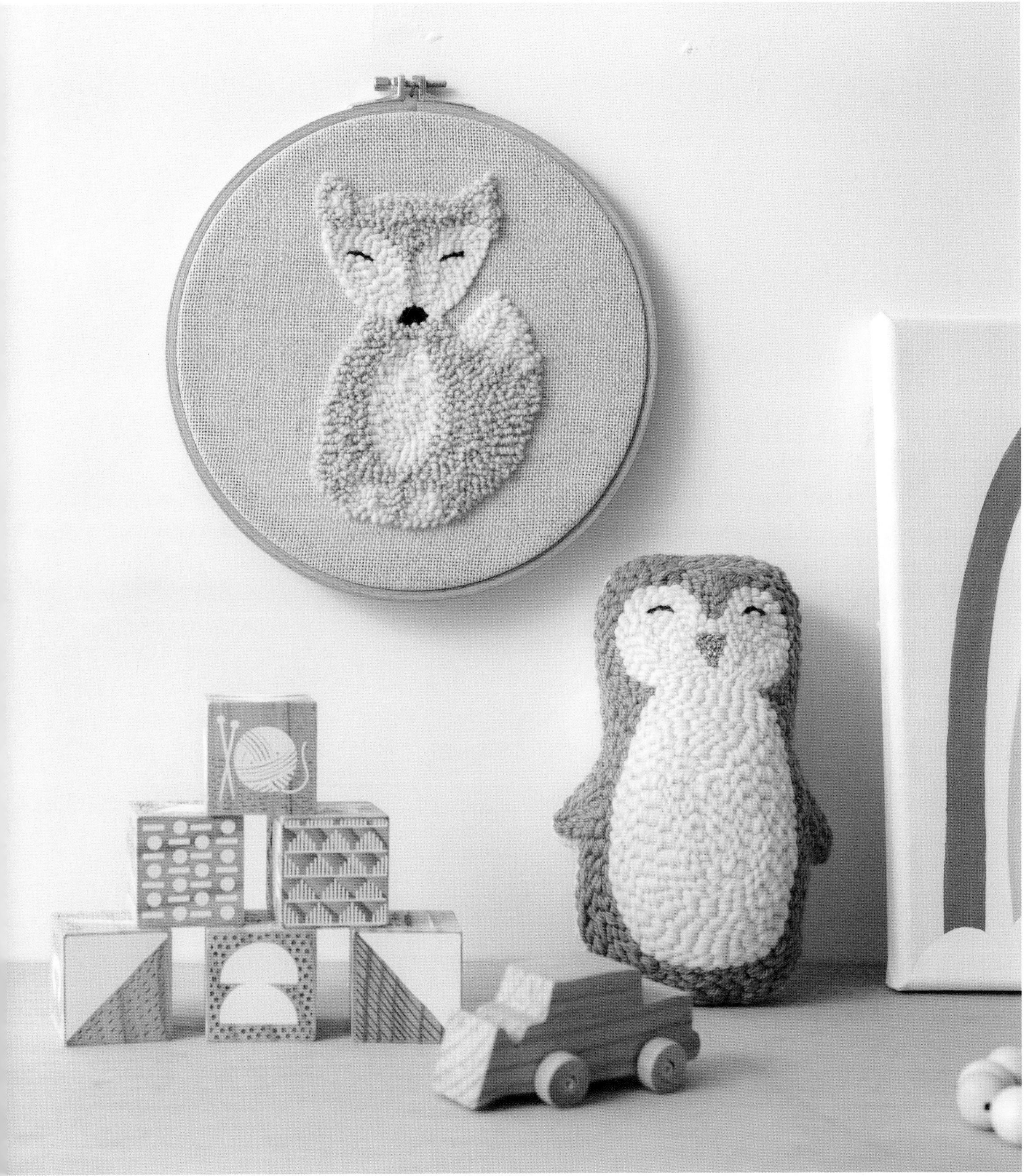

Instructions

1. Follow Steps 1-3, page 15, of Hoop Wall Hanging to place the fabric in the embroidery hoop.

2. Transfer the pattern (page 71) to the fabric. It is not necessary to transfer the dashes and circles.

3. Referring to the table and photo, work the detail flat stitches from the front side of the fabric for the eye and nose. Work the remaining flat stitches from the front side of the fabric and the loop stitches from the back side of the fabric.

Yarn	Needle	Stitch	Side of Fabric
Black (B)	#14 mini	Flat	Front
Off-White (OW)	#14 mini	Flat	Front
Grey (G)	#14 mini	Loop	Back
Off-White (OW)	#14 mini	Loop	Back

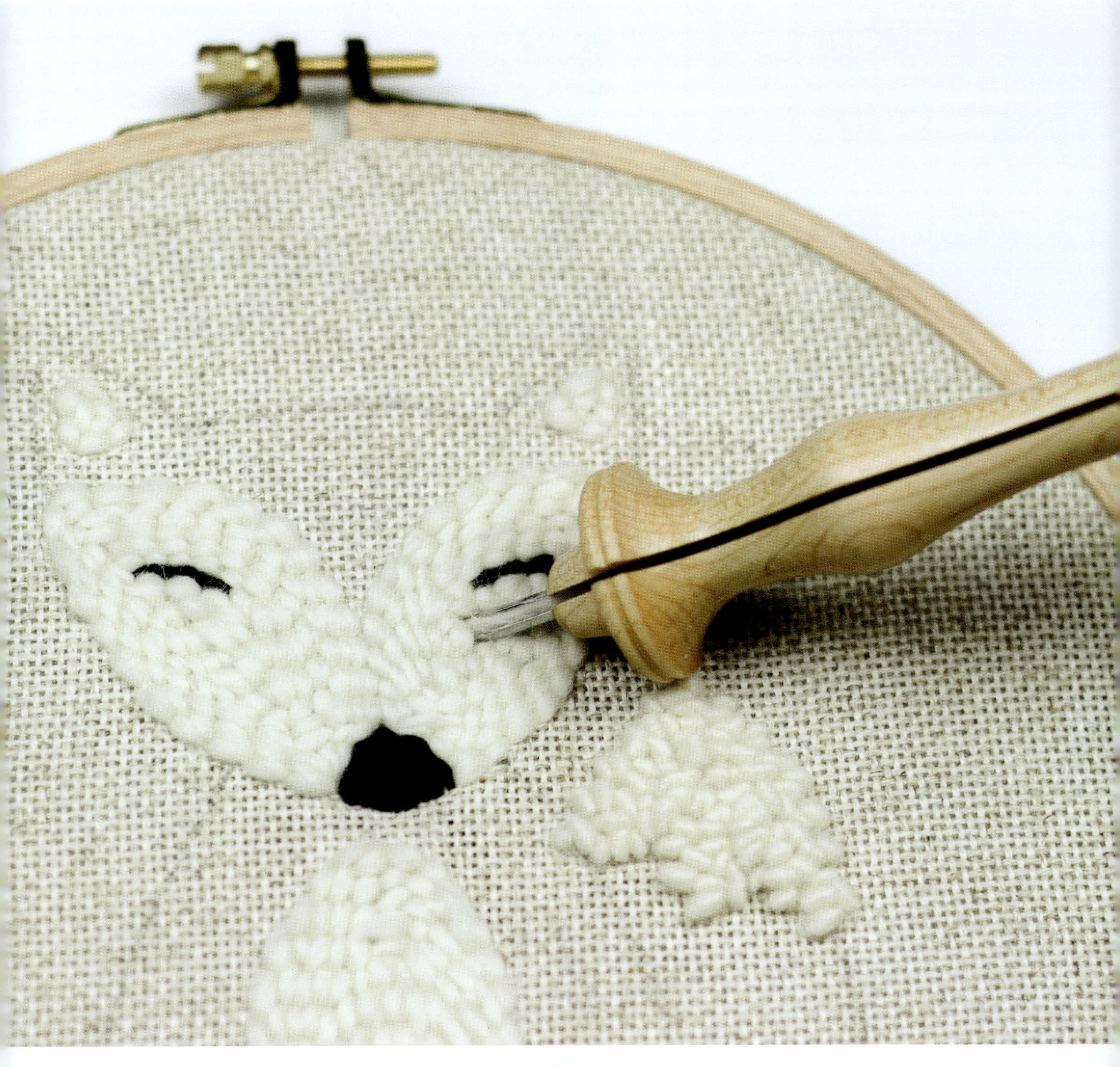

Mermaid Pouch

SHOPPING LIST

- Oxford Punch Needles: #10 regular and #14 mini

- 12" x 12" piece of 18 count Floba

- 8" diameter non-slip embroidery hoop

- 5" zipper

- 8" x 8" piece of fabric for pouch back

- 8" x 16" piece of fabric for pouch lining

- 6" x 7" piece of lightweight woven fusible interfacing

- Size 5 Bulky Weight yarn
  4 yards blue-grey
  15 yards off-white

- Size 4 Medium Weight yarn
  6 yards blue
  7 yards metallic gold

- Sewing thread to match Floba fabric

- Sewing machine with zipper foot

29

Instructions

Unless otherwise noted, always match right sides and raw edges when sewing.

Yarn	Needle	Stitch	Side of Fabric
Off-White (OW)	#10 regular	Flat	Front
Blue-Grey (BG)	#10 regular	Flat	Front
Blue (B)	#10 regular	Flat	Front
Metallic Gold (MG)	#14 mini	Flat	Front

1. For the pouch front, place the Floba fabric in the hoop, making sure it is drum-tight in the hoop. Transfer the pattern (page 72) to the fabric. It is not necessary to transfer the dashes and circles.

2. Referring to the table and photo, work the flat stitches from the front side of the fabric. Remove the hoop and trim the fabric ½" from the design. This will be the seam allowance.

3. Trim the interfacing to the shape of the stitched area. Follow the manufacturer's instructions to fuse the interfacing to the loops on the back side of the pouch front.

4. Using the pouch front as a pattern, cut 2 lining pieces and a pouch back piece. Set back piece aside for now. Attach the zipper foot to the sewing machine. Open the zipper. Place the zipper, right side against the pouch front, matching the zipper ends to the corners of the stitching. Matching the raw edges, place one lining piece right side down over the zipper and the pouch front. Sew the pieces together along the straight edge, stitching close to the zipper teeth.

5. Turn the lining to the wrong side and press the straight edge of the pouch.

6. Repeat Steps 4-5 with the pouch back and the remaining lining piece.

7. With the zipper still open, turn out and pin the lining pieces right sides together. Pin the pouch front and back together. Leaving a 3" opening in the lining, sew the pieces together.

8. Turn the pouch right side out through the opening in the lining.

9. Press the raw edges of the lining opening to the wrong side and pin closed; hand sew the opening closed. Push the lining into the pouch and zip closed.

Pin Trio

SHOPPING LIST

- Ultra-Punch® Needle

- 11" x 11" piece of tightly woven cotton fabric

- 6" x 6" piece of pearl-white faux leather fabric

- 7" diameter non-slip embroidery hoop

- 3 25mm round flat pin backs

- Size 1 Super Fine Weight
    cotton yarn
  7 yards mustard
  7 yards off-white
  5 yards dark green
  4 yards metallic copper
  4 yards light rose
  4 yards peach
  3 yards teal

- Hot glue gun and glue sticks

33

Instructions

1. Place the fabric in the hoop, making sure it is drum-tight in the hoop. Transfer the patterns (page 72) to the fabric. It is not necessary to transfer the circles.

2. Referring to the tables and photo, work loop stitches from the back side of the fabric.

Brooch 1

Yarn	Ultra Punch Needle Position	Stitch	Side of Fabric
Mustard (M)	5	Loop	Back
Off-White (OW)	8	Loop	Back
Dark Green (DG)	6	Loop	Back

Brooch 2

Yarn	Ultra Punch Needle Position	Stitch	Side of Fabric
Metallic Copper (MC)	8	Loop	Back
Light Rose (LR)	4	Loop	Back
Peach (P)	4	Loop	Back

Brooch 3

Yarn	Ultra Punch Needle Position	Stitch	Side of Fabric
Teal (T)	6	Loop	Back
Mustard (M)	8	Loop	Back
Off-White (OW)	5	Loop	Back

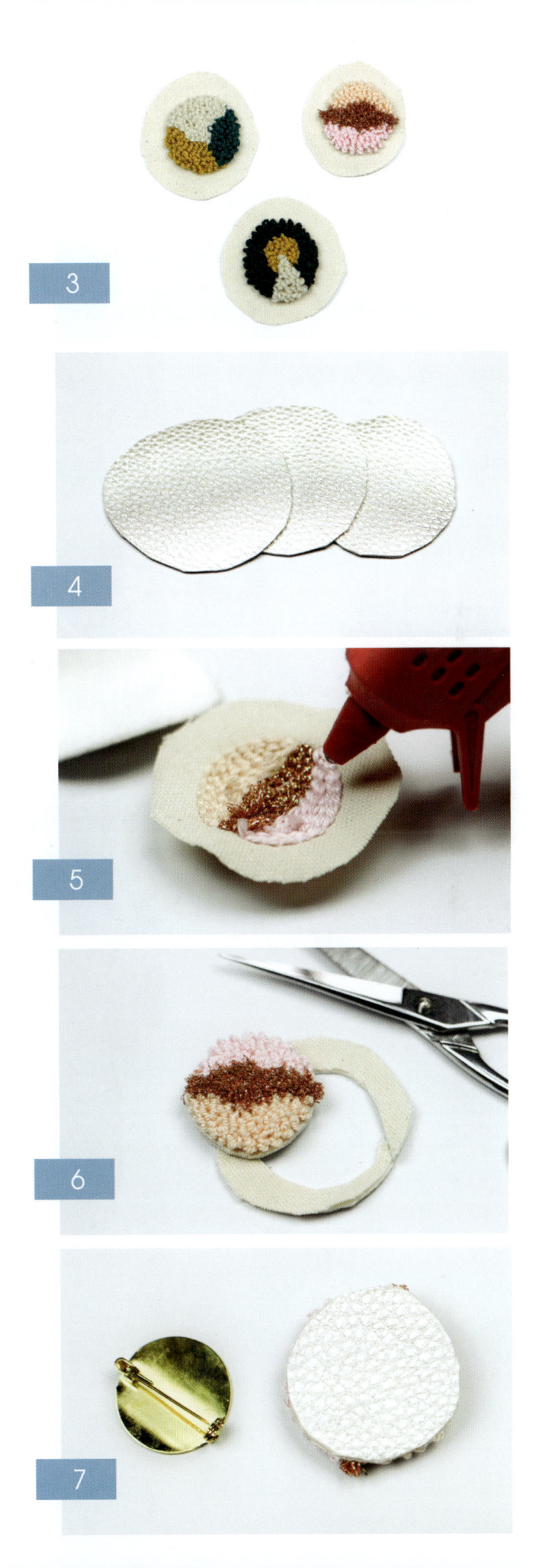

3. Remove the hoop and trim each stitched piece to 1" from outer edges of design.

4. Cut a circle of faux leather the same size as each stitched circle.

5. Matching the wrong sides, glue a faux leather circle to each stitched circle.

6. Trim the excess fabric and faux leather from each design, cutting close to, but not through the stitching.

7. Glue a flat pin back to the faux leather on each pin.

Floral Duo

SHOPPING LIST

- Oxford Punch Needle: #14 fine

- 16" x 16" piece of 18 count Floba fabric

- 12" diameter non-slip embroidery hoop

- 2 4" x 6" pieces of heavy cardboard or mat board

- 2 3¾" x 5¾" pieces of cardstock for backing

- Size 4 Medium Weight yarn
  16 yards black
  5 yards metallic copper
  5 yards coral

- Hot glue gun and glue sticks

37

Instructions

1. Place the fabric in the hoop, making sure it is drum-tight in the hoop. Transfer the patterns (page 74) to the fabric, spacing them about 4" apart. It is not necessary to transfer the dashes and circles.

2. Referring to the table and photo, work the flat stitches from the front side of the fabric and the loop stitches from the back side of the fabric. After stitching is complete, trim each design to 5½" x 7½", centering the stitched design.

3. Center the cardboard pieces on the back side of the stitched pieces; glue the cardboard to the fabric.

Yarn	Needle	Stitch	Side of Fabric
Black (BK)	#14 fine	Flat	Front
Metallic Copper (MC)	#14 fine	Loop	Back
Coral (C)	#14 fine	Loop	Back

38 www.leisurearts.com

4. To miter to fabric corners, trim the excess fabric at the corners. Fold and glue the fabric edges to the cardboard.

5. For the backing, center and glue the cardstock pieces to the cardboard.

39

Denim Jacket

SHOPPING LIST

- Ultra-Punch® Needle

- Black denim jacket

- 7" diameter non-slip embroidery hoop

- Six strand cotton embroidery floss
  2 yards black
  17 yards red
  4 yards dark red
  4 yards green
  4 yards light green

- 7" x 4½" piece of lightweight woven fusible interfacing

- White or yellow transfer paper

- Tracing paper

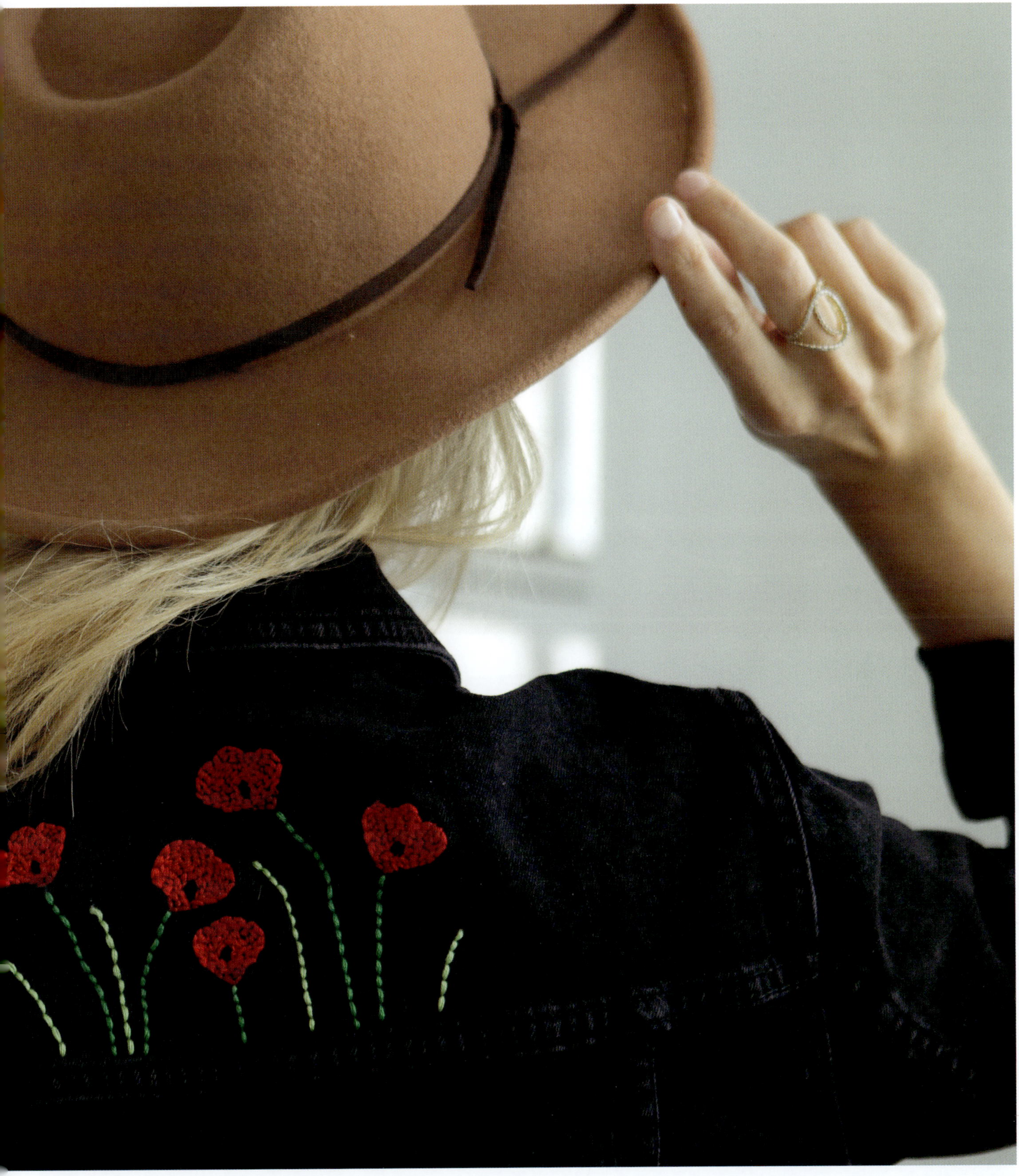

Instructions

1. Place the jacket yoke in the hoop, making sure it is drum-tight in the hoop.

2. Trace the pattern (page 75) onto tracing paper. Placing the transfer paper between the pattern and the jacket, position the pattern on the jacket back yoke. Draw over the pattern with a blunt pencil. It is not necessary to transfer the dashes.

3. Referring to the table and photo, work the flat stitches from the front side of the jacket.

4. Trim any excess or long threads from inside the jacket.

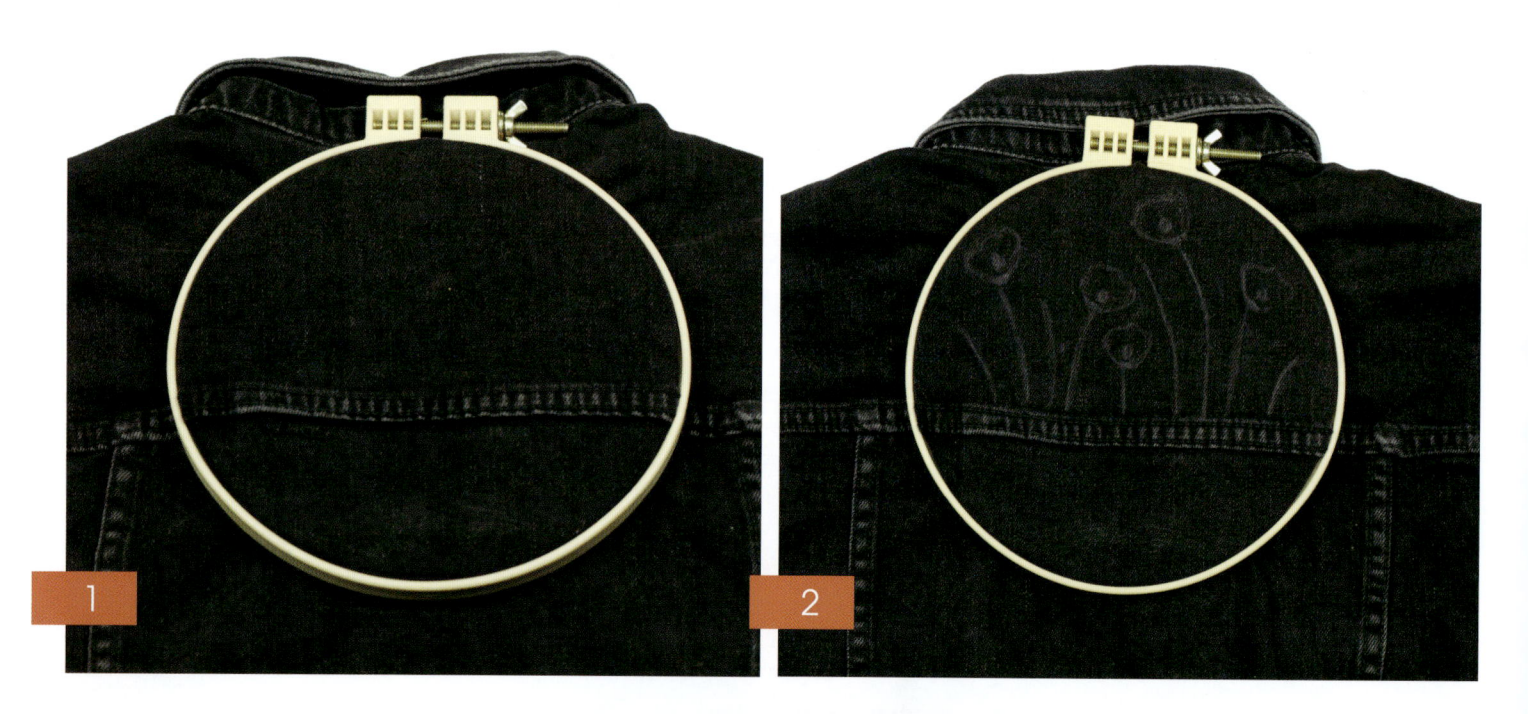

4

5

Embroidery Floss	Ultra Punch Needle Position	Stitch	Side of Fabric
Black (BK)	7	Flat	Front
Red (R)	7	Flat	Front
Dark Red (DR)	7	Flat	Front
Green (G)	7	Flat	Front
Light Green (LG)	7	Flat	Front

5. Follow the manufacturer's instructions to fuse the interfacing to the loops on the inside of the jacket.

Purse

SHOPPING LIST

- Oxford Punch Needle: #10 regular and #10 fine

- 2 pieces of Monk's cloth fabric (20" x 20" and 16" x 16")

- 16" x 16" tube and clamp frame

- 12" diameter non-slip embroidery hoop

- 1¼ yards metallic gold cording for strap

- Size 18 tapestry needle

- Hand sewing needle and thread to match off-white yarn

- Size 5 Bulky Weight yarn
  171 yards off-white
  21 yards blue-grey
  22 yards peach

- Size 4 Medium Weight yarn
  42 yards teal

- Sew-on magnetic snap

- Clover Wonder Clips

44   www.leisurearts.com

Instructions

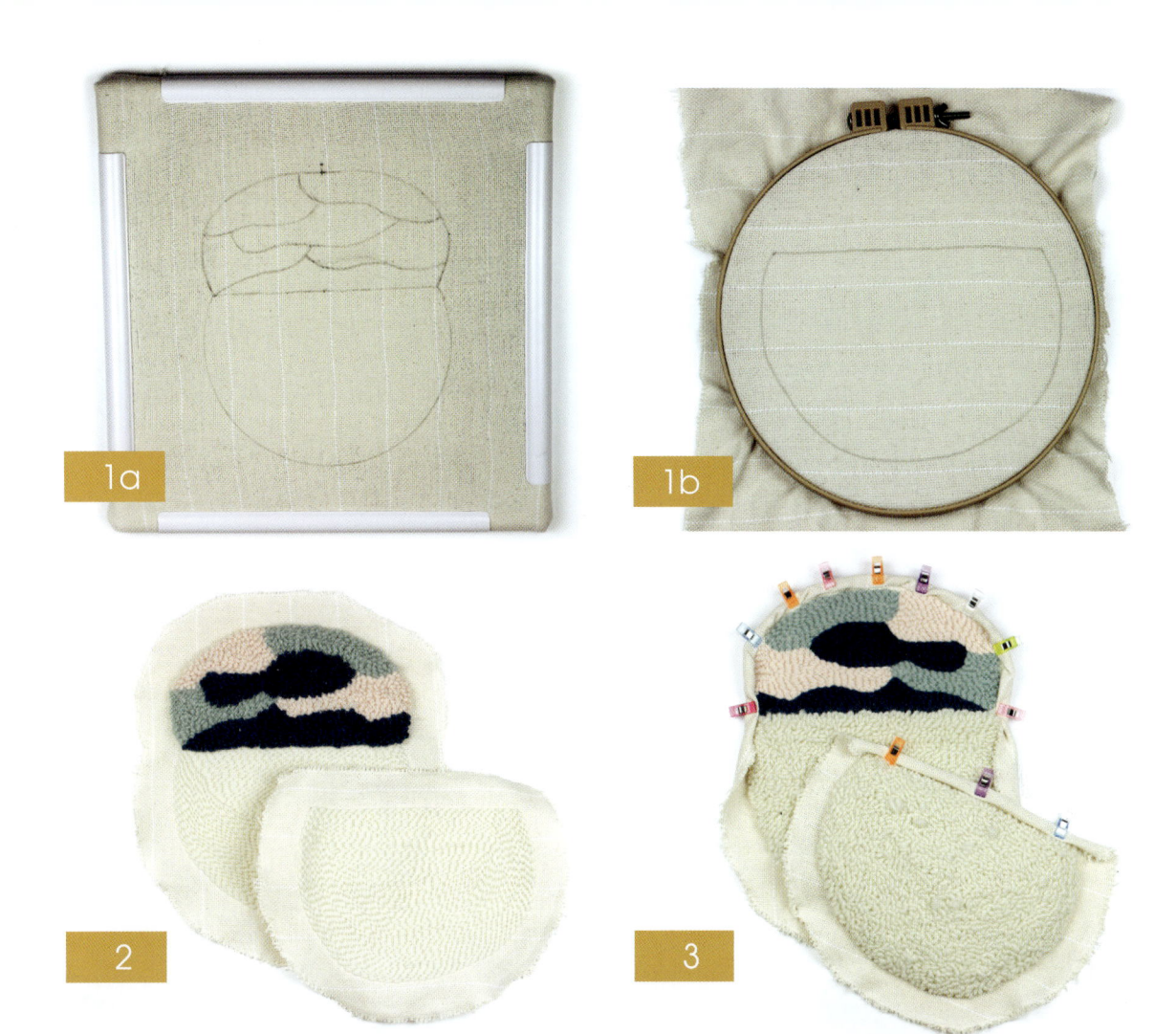

1. Place the larger fabric piece in the frame, making sure it is drum-tight in the frame. Place the smaller fabric piece in the hoop, making sure it is drum-tight in the hoop. Transfer the entire pattern (page 76) to the fabric in the frame. Transfer the solid half only to the fabric in the hoop. It is not necessary to transfer the dashes and circles.

2. Referring to the table and photo, work the flat stitches from the front side of the fabric and the loop stitches from the back side of the fabric. Remove the frame and the hoop. Trim the stitched pieces to 1½" from the outer edges of designs. Zigzag stitch all the fabric edges.

3. Roll the seam allowance on the stitched flap and the purse front to the back side and secure with Wonder Clips.

Yarn	Needle	Stitch	Side of Fabric
Off-White (OW)	#10 regular	Flat	Front
Blue-Grey (BG)	#10 regular	Loop	Back
Peach (P)	#10 regular	Loop	Back
Teal (T)	#10 fine	Loop	Back

45

4. Thread the tapestry needle with off-white yarn. Leaving a 2" tail, insert the needle from the back side to the front side, right above the stitched area at one end of the purse front.

5. Bring the needle over the rolled edge and insert it right next to the previous insertion point; pull the needle and yarn through. Repeat across to the opposite side, covering the beginning tail as you sew.

6. After you take the last stitch on the opposite end, pass the needle under several stitches and pull tautly. Cut the yarn flush with the stitches.

46   www.leisurearts.com

7. Using matching yarn, repeat Steps 4-6 to cover the edges of the purse flap. Roll and join the purse edges together in the same manner.

8. Hand sew the snap to the flap and purse front.

9. For the strap, hand sew the cord to the upper corners of the purse.

10. Using yarn that matches the purse flap when it is closed, cover cord ends.

Penguin Toy

SHOPPING LIST

- Oxford Punch Needles: #10 regular and #10 fine

- 16" x 16" piece of Monk's cloth fabric

- 9" x 12" piece of fabric for back

- 7" x 10" piece of lightweight woven fusible interfacing

- 12" diameter non-slip embroidery hoop

- Size 5 Bulky Weight yarn
  30 yards off-white

- Size 4 Medium Weight yarn
  1 yard black
  1 yard metallic gold
  36 yards blue

- Sewing thread to match Monk's cloth fabric

- Hand sewing needle

- Polyester fiberfill

- Sewing machine

48 www.leisurearts.com

49

Instructions

Unless otherwise noted, always match right sides and raw edges when sewing.

1. Place the fabric in the hoop, making sure it is drum tight in the hoop. Transfer the pattern (page 77) to the fabric. It is not necessary to transfer the dashes.

2. Referring to the table and photo, work flat stitches from the front side of the fabric, stitching the eyes and beak first.

Yarn	Needle	Stitch	Side of Fabric
Black (BK)	#10 fine	Flat	Front
Metallic Gold (MG)	#10 fine	Flat	Front
Off-White (OW)	#10 regular	Flat	Front
Blue (B)	#10 regular	Flat	Front

3. Remove the hoop and trim the stitched piece to ¾" from outer edge of design. Cut the fusible interfacing to the shape of the stitched penguin. Follow the manufacturer's instructions to fuse the interfacing to the loops on the back side.

4. Cut the back fabric the same size and shape as the front stitched piece. Pin together along the edges. Leaving the bottom for turning, sew the penguin front and back together, sewing about ¼" from the stitched areas.

50   www.leisurearts.com

5. Carefully clip the seam allowances at the corners and curves. Turn the penguin right side out.

6. Stuff the penguin with fiberfill.

7. Turn the fabric raw edges to the inside and hand sew the opening closed.

Coaster Set

SHOPPING LIST

- Oxford Punch Needle: #10 regular

- 16" x 16" piece of monk's cloth fabric

- 12" diameter non-slip embroidery hoop

- 2 4" x 4" squares of felt for backing

- Size 5 Bulky Weight yarn
  10 yards peach
  10 yards rust
  7 yards eggshell cotton
  8 yards mustard
  9 yards plum cotton
  10 yards mauve
  10 yards aqua cotton

- Hand sewing thread to match Monk's cloth fabric

- Hand sewing needle

- Hot glue gun and glue sticks

www.leisurearts.com

53

Instructions

1. Place the fabric in the hoop, making sure it is drum-tight in the hoop. Transfer the patterns (page 78) to the fabric, placing the designs about 2" apart. It is not necessary to transfer the circles.

2. Referring to the table and photo, work loop stitches from the back side of the fabric.

3. Push any yarn ends on the back side of the fabric to the loop side of the fabric.

4. Trim the stitched piece to ¾" from the outer edges of the design. You will turn this under.

Yarn	Needle	Stitch	Side of Fabric
Peach (P)	#10 regular	Loop	Back
Rust (R)	#10 regular	Loop	Back
Eggshell (E)	#10 regular	Loop	Back
Mustard (MD)	#10 regular	Loop	Back
Plum (PL)	#10 regular	Loop	Back
Mauve (M)	#10 regular	Loop	Back
Aqua (A)	#10 regular	Loop	Back

54 www.leisurearts.com

5. Fold the raw fabric edges to the back side of the fabric. You can press them with an iron.

6. Tack the corners in place.

7. Glue a felt piece to the back of each coaster.

Rectangular Pillow

SHOPPING LIST

- Oxford Punch Needle: #10 regular and #10 fine

- 21" x 15" piece of 18 count Floba fabric

- 17" x 12" piece of fabric for pillow back

- 17" x 11" tube and clamp frame

- 15½" x 9" piece of lightweight woven fusible interfacing

- Polyester fiberfill

- Size 5 Bulky Weight yarn
  18 yards peach
  15 yards mustard
  17 yards eggshell cotton
  22 yards cream/navy speckled cotton
  22 yards off-white

- Size 4 Medium Weight yarn
  29 yards blue-grey
  47 yards coral

- Appliqué scissors

- Sewing machine

- Hand sewing needle

- Sewing thread to match Floba fabric

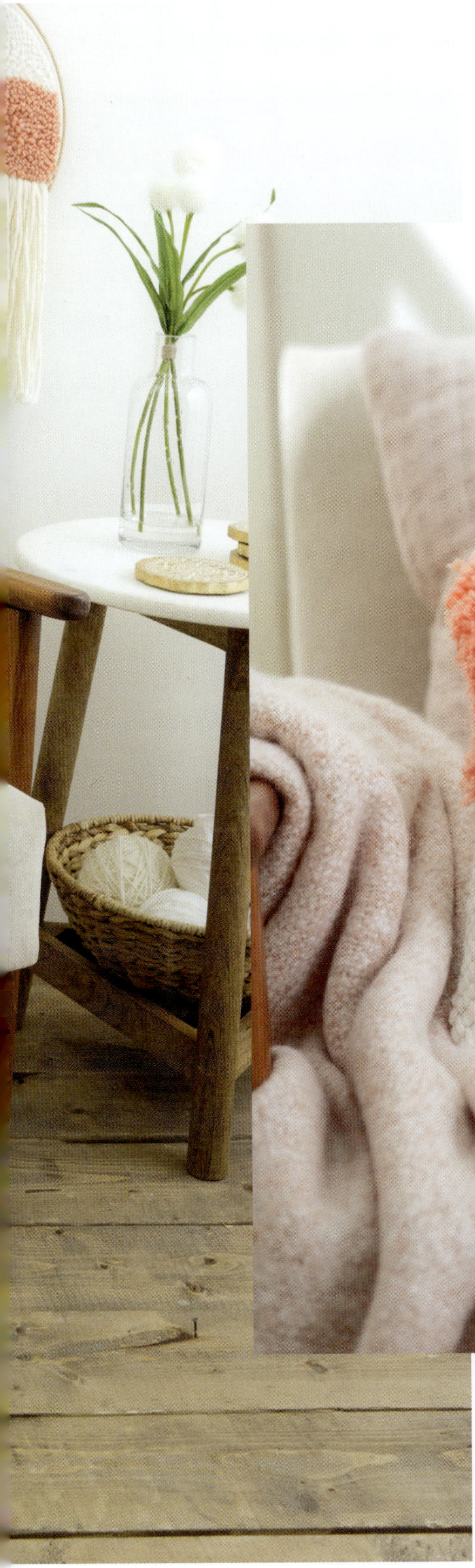
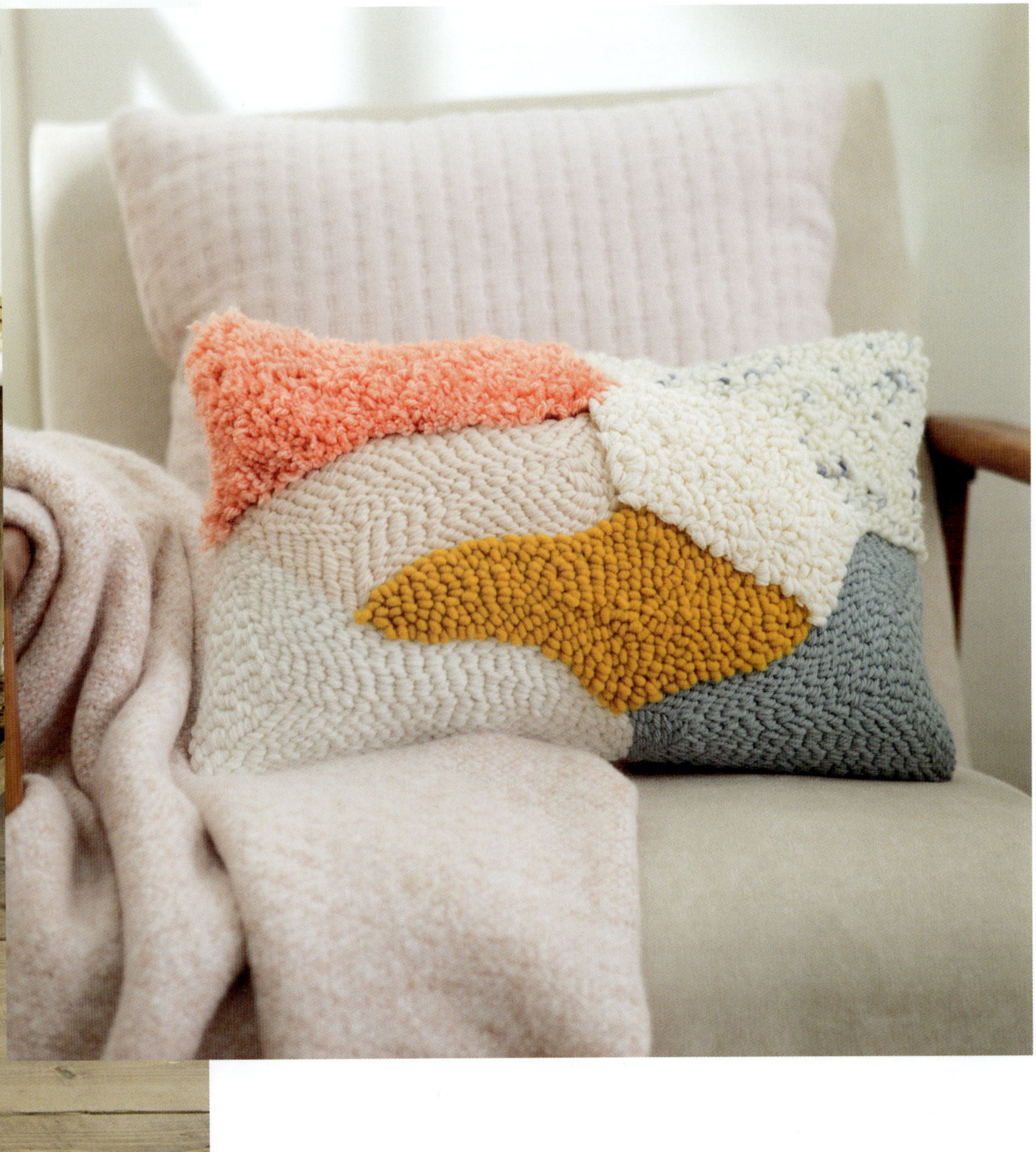

1

2

3

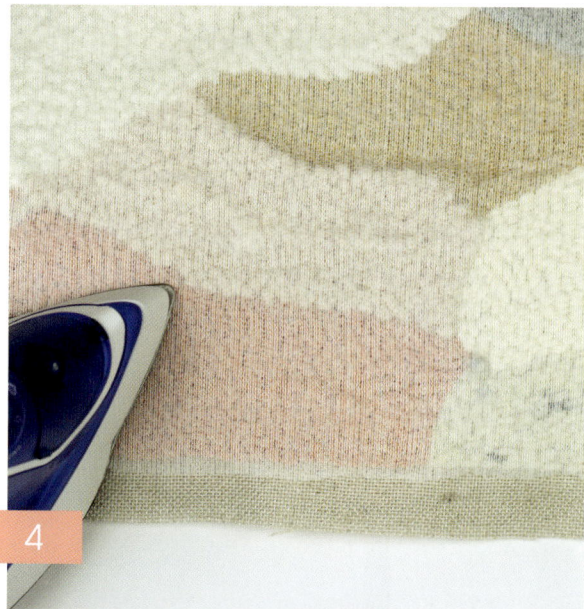

4

5

58 www.leisurearts.com

Instructions

Unless otherwise noted, always match right sides and raw edges when sewing.

Yarn	Needle	Stitch	Side of Fabric
Blue-Grey (BG)	#10 fine	Flat	Front
Off-White (OW)	#10 regular	Flat	Front
Peach (P)	#10 regular	Flat	Front
Mustard (MD)	#10 regular	Loop	Back
Eggshell (E)	#10 regular	Loop	Back
Cream/Navy Speckled (CN)	#10 regular	Loop	Back
Coral (C)	#10 regular (use 2 strands of yarn)	Shag	Back

1. Place the Floba fabric in the frame, making sure it is drum-tight in the frame. Transfer the pattern (page 79) to the fabric in the frame. It is not necessary to transfer the dashes and circles.

2. Referring to the table and photo, work the flat stitches from the front side of the fabric and the loop and shag stitches from the back side of the fabric. Trim the coral loops with the appliqué scissors. Trim any yarn ends.

3. Remove the frame. Trim the stitched piece to 1" from the stitched area. This will be your seam allowance.

4. Follow the manufacturer's instructions to fuse the interfacing to the back side of the fabric.

5. Leaving a 4" opening on the bottom for turning, sew the stitched fabric and the pillow back together.

6. Clip the corners and trim the seam allowances to ½".

7. Turn the pillow right side out and stuff with fiberfill.

8. Turn the fabric raw edges to the inside and hand sew the opening closed.

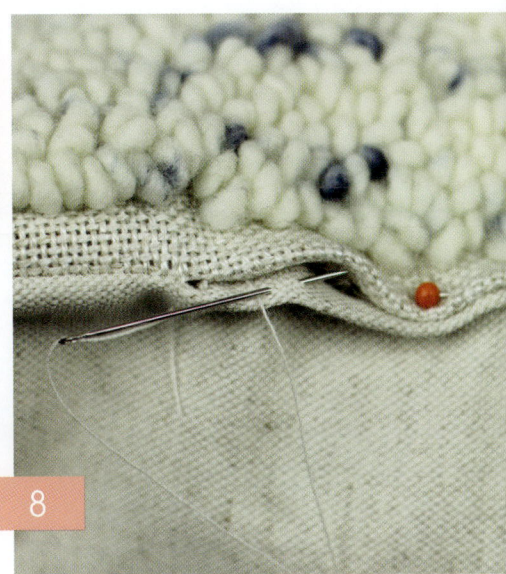

6

7

8

59

Storage Pouch

SHOPPING LIST

- Oxford Punch Needle: #10 regular

- 22" x 15" piece of 18 count Floba fabric

- 17" x 11" tube and clamp frame

- 22" x 15" piece of fabric for lining

- 3¼" x 15¾" piece of lightweight woven fusible interfacing

- Size 5 Bulky Weight yarn
  12 yards peach
  10 yards rust
  11 yards yellow
  32 yards off-white

- Sewing machine

- Sewing thread to match Floba fabric

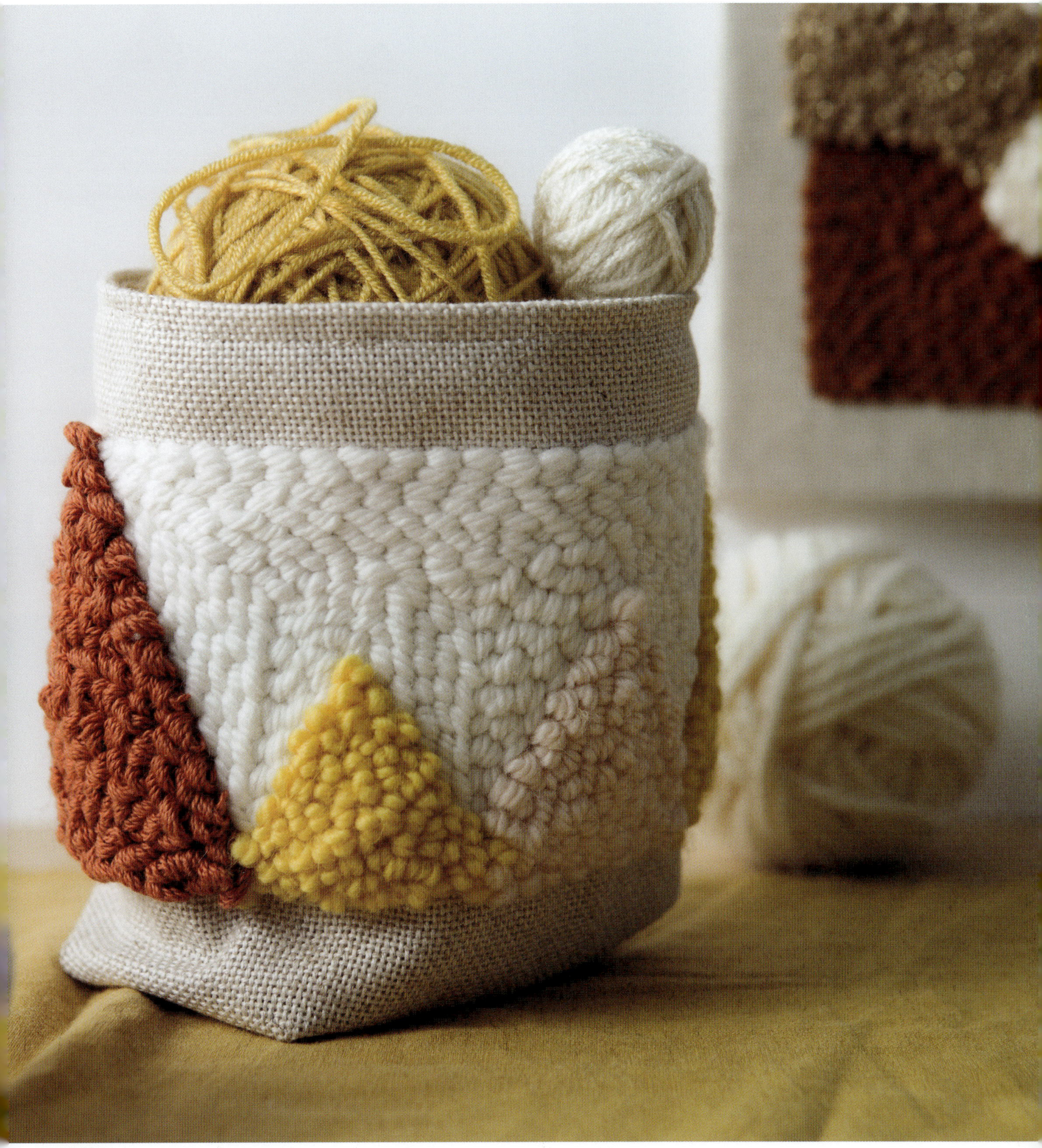

Instructions

Unless otherwise noted, always match right sides and raw edges when sewing.

1. Place the fabric in the frame, making sure it is drum-tight in the frame. Transfer the pattern (page 73) to the fabric. It is not necessary to transfer the dashes and circles.

2. Referring to the table and photo, work the flat stitches from the front side of the fabric and the loop stitches from the back side of the fabric.

3. Remove the frame and trim the stitched piece to 1" away from the outer drawn lines. This will be the seam allowance.

4. Follow the manufacturer's instructions to fuse the interfacing to the back side of the stitched piece.

5. Matching the short ends, fold the stitched piece in half and pin the sides and bottom together. Sew the sides and bottom together, stitching on the drawn lines. Be sure to leave the top open.

62 www.leisurearts.com

Yarn	Needle	Stitch	Side of Fabric
Off-White (OW)	#10 regular	Flat	Front
Peach (P)	#10 regular	Loop	Back
Yellow (Y)	#10 regular	Loop	Back
Rust (R)	#10 regular	Loop	Back

6. Flatten the bottom of the container on your work surface. Pin across the points of the fabric. Sew together 1½" from the point, sewing through all layers. Trim the excess fabric.

7. Draw the seamlines on the lining fabric. Repeat Steps 5-6 with the lining fabric.

8. Turn the storage pouch right side out. Place the lining inside the pouch; match the seams and the top edges.

9. Turn the raw edges of both the lining and the stitched piece ½" to the wrong side and pin. Topstitch close to the edge, stitching through all fabric layers.

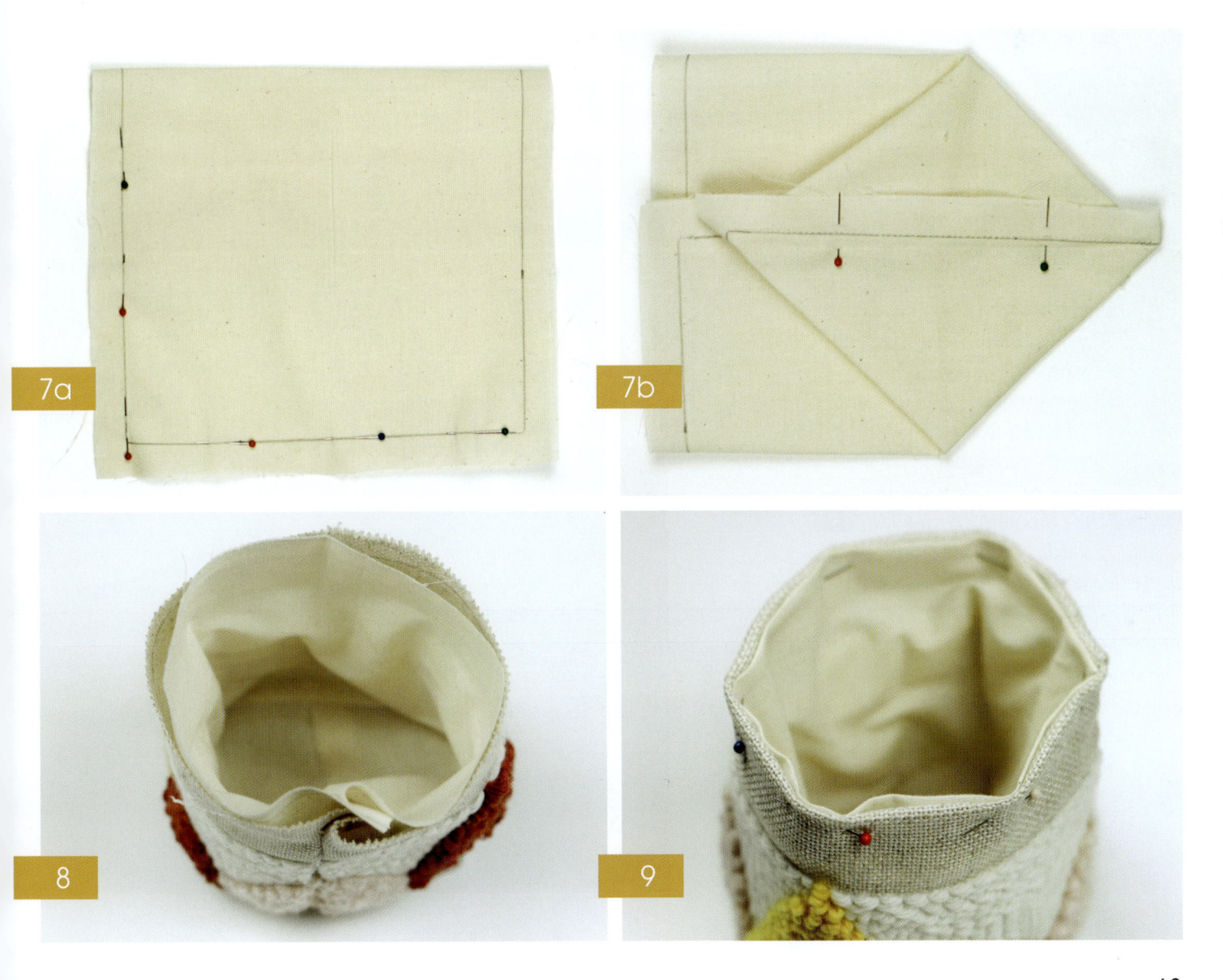

7a

7b

8

9

63

Round Pouf

SHOPPING LIST

- Oxford Punch Needles: #10 fine and #10 regular

- 27" x 27" piece of 18 count Floba fabric

- 23" diameter quilting hoop

- 23" diameter piece of fabric for pouf back

- 20" diameter piece of woven lightweight fusible interfacing

- Size 5 Bulky Weight yarn
  65 yards eggshell cotton
  42 yards yellow
  31 yards peach
  29 yards blue-grey
  50 yards cream/navy speckled
  23 yards light grey
  33 yards mauve
  27 yards aqua cotton
  75 yards dark green

- Size 4 Medium Weight yarn
  25 yards metallic gold
  12 yards white/navy speckled

- Polyester fiberfill

- Hand sewing needle

- Sewing machine

- Sewing thread to match Floba fabric

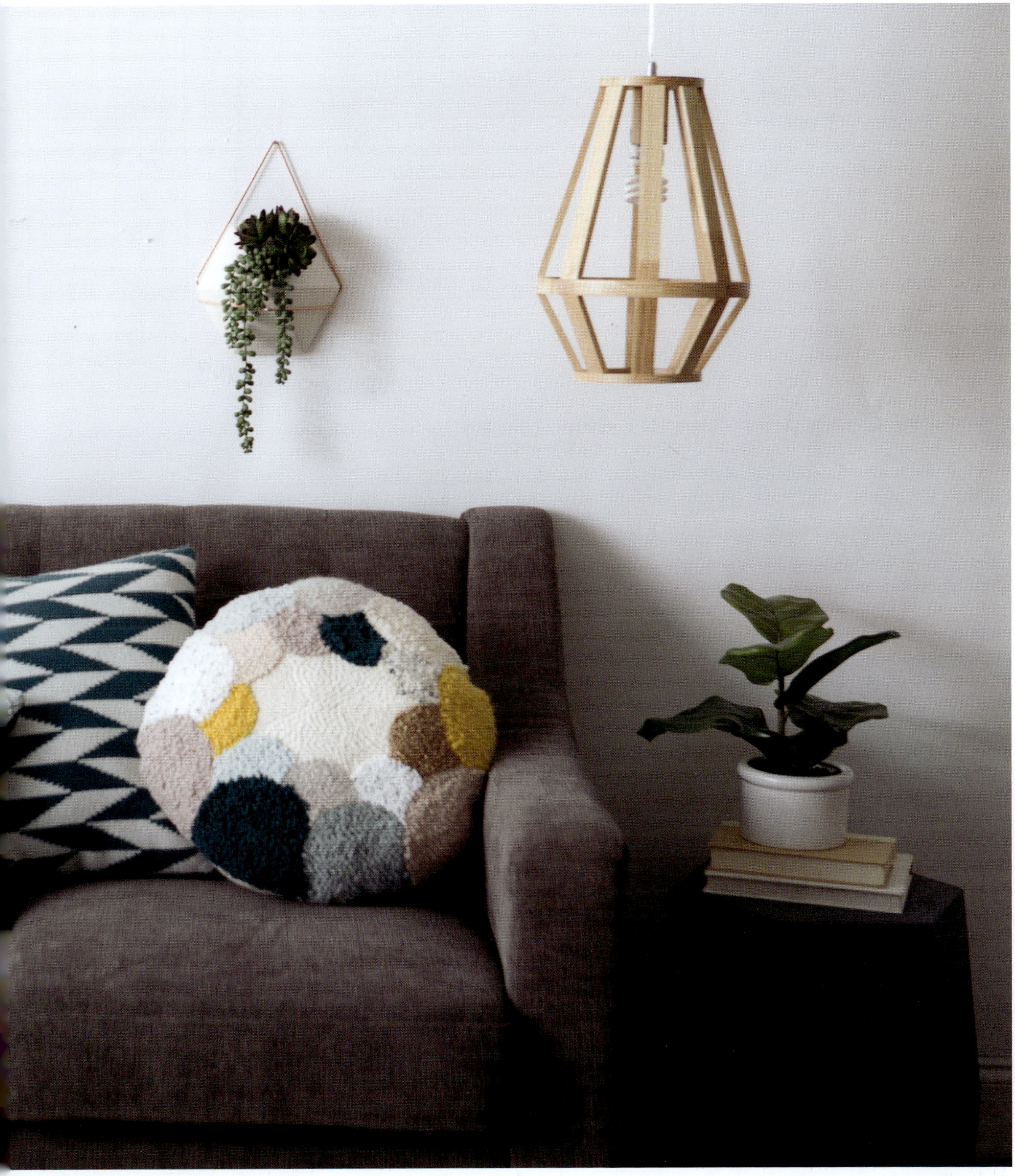

Instructions

Unless otherwise noted, always match right sides and raw edges when sewing.

1. Place the fabric in the hoop, making sure it is drum-tight in the hoop. Transfer the pattern (page 80) to the fabric. It is not necessary to transfer the dashes and circles.

Yarn	Needle	Stitch	Side of Fabric
Eggshell (E)	#10 regular	Flat	Front
Metallic Gold (MG)	#10 fine	Loop	Back
Yellow (Y)	#10 regular	Loop	Back
Peach (P)	#10 regular	Loop	Back
Speckled White/Navy (WN)	#10 fine	Loop	Back
Blue-Grey (BG)	#10 regular	Loop	Back
Speckled Cream/Navy (CN)	#10 regular	Loop	Back
Light Grey (LG)	#10 regular	Loop	Back
Mauve (M)	#10 regular	Loop	Back
Aqua (A)	#10 regular	Loop	Back
Dark Green (DG)	#10 regular	Loop	Back
Eggshell (E)	#10 regular	Loop	Back

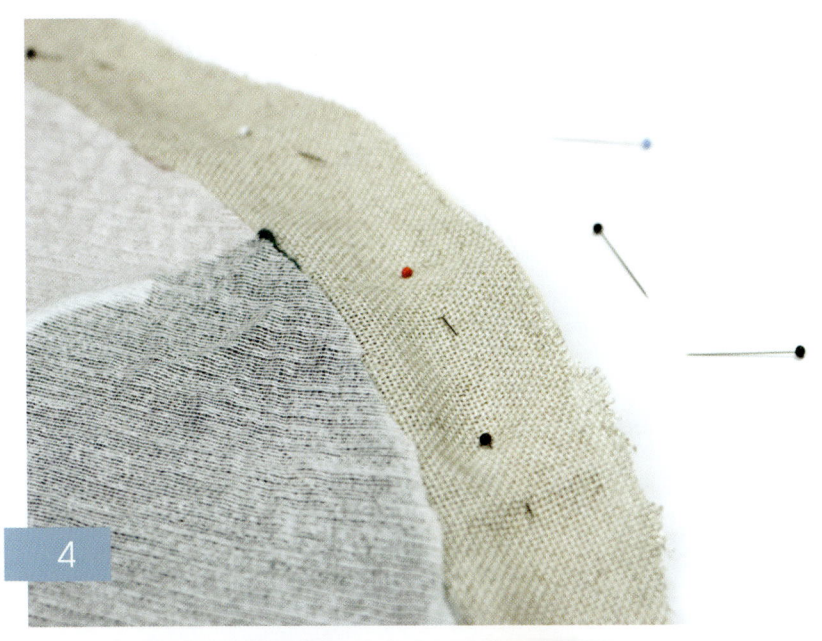

2. Referring to the table and photo, work the flat stitches from the front side of the fabric and the loop stitches from the back side of the fabric.

3. Remove the frame. Trim the stitched piece to 1½" from the stitched area. This will be your seam allowance. Follow the manufacturer's instructions to fuse the interfacing to the back side of the fabric.

4. Zigzag stitch a 6" area along the edge of both the stitched fabric and the pouf back. Matching the zigzagged areas, pin the stitched fabric and pouf back together. Sewing about ½" from the stitched area and leaving the zigzagged area open for turning and stuffing, sew the pieces together.

5. Trim the excess fabric to ½"; clip curves as necessary. Turn the pouf right side out and firmly stuff with fiberfill.

6. Turn the zigzagged edges to the inside and hand sew the opening closed.

Patterns

Hoop Wall Hanging

— = Flat Stitch
○ = Loop Stitch
P = Peach
M = Mustard
GG = Grey-Green
MG = Metallic Gold
WN = White/Navy Speckled

Photocopy Hoop pattern at 118%

Leisure Arts, Inc. grants permission to the owner of this book to make photocopies of the patterns on pages 68-80 for personal use only.

Fringed Wall Hanging

— = Flat Stitch
○ = Loop Stitch
P = Peach
M = Mustard
OW = Off-White
PL = Plum
C = Coral

Photocopy Wall Hanging pattern at 200%
Do not trace grey line.

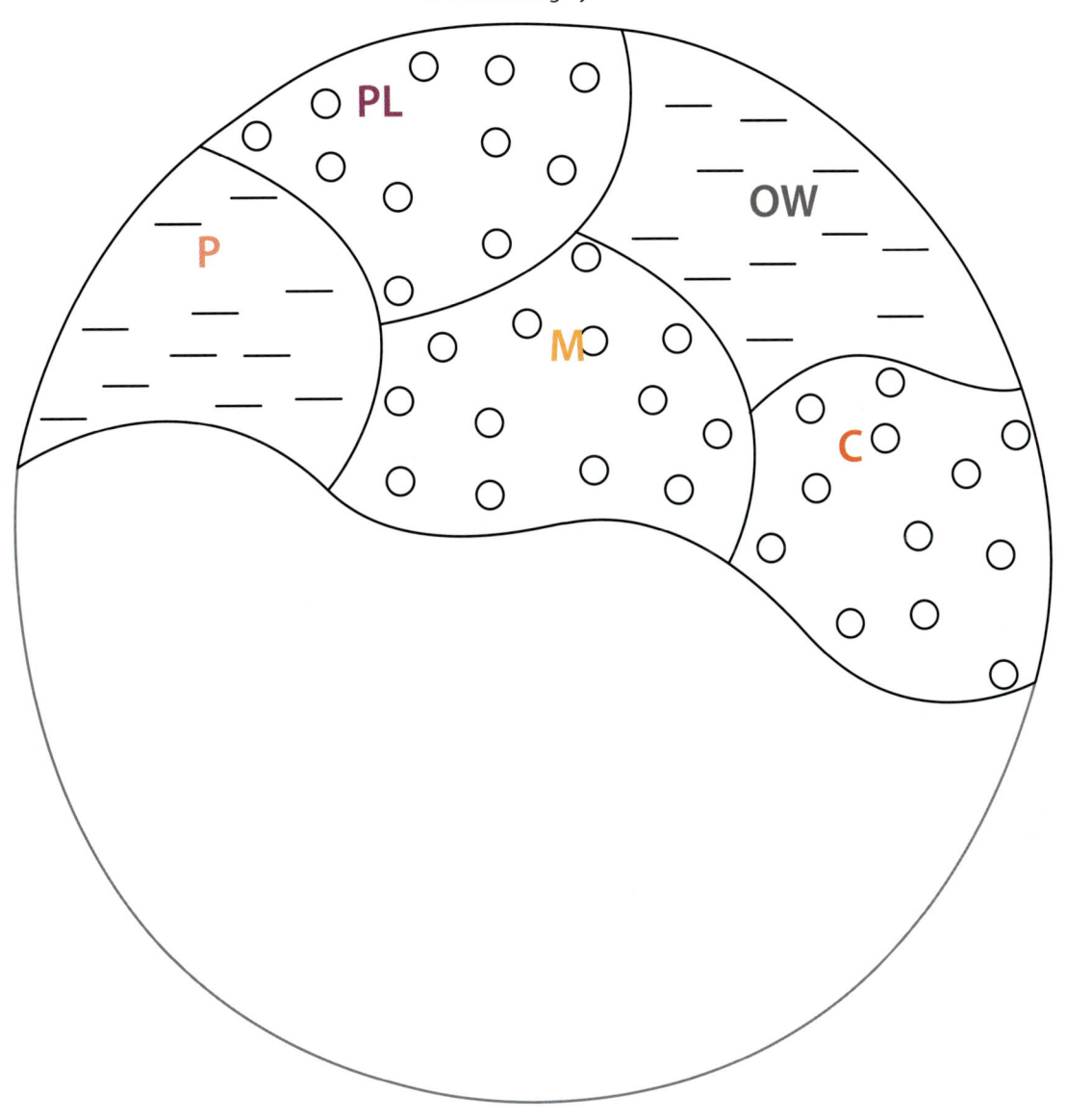

69

Abstract Landscape Frame

— = Flat Stitch M = Mustard
O = Loop Stitch R = Rust
X = Shag Stitch MG = Metallic Gold
P = Peach E = Eggshell

Photocopy Landscape pattern at 121%.
Do not trace grey lines.

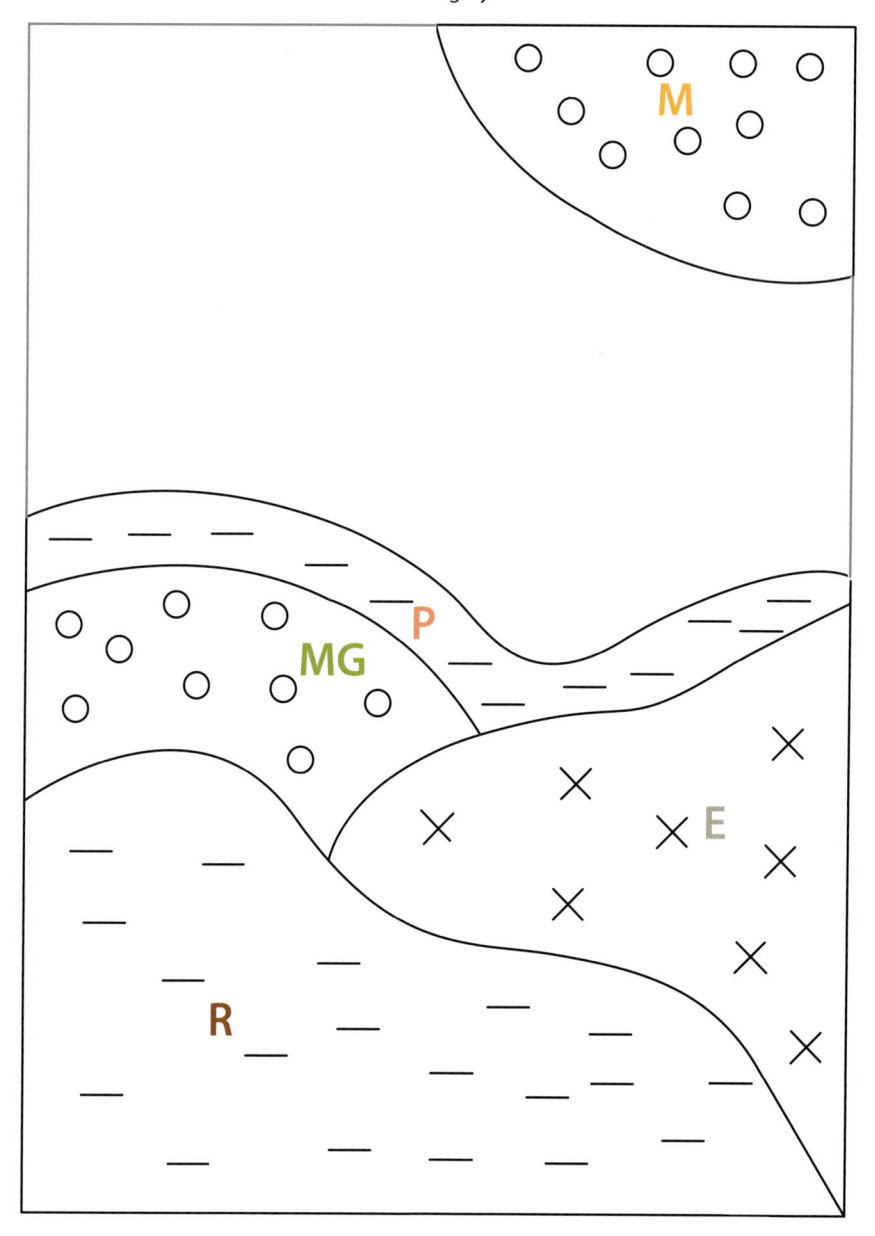

70 www.leisurearts.com

Arctic Fox Wall Hanging

——— = Flat Stitch
◯ = Loop Stitch
B = Black
G = Grey
OW = Off-White

Fox pattern is full size.

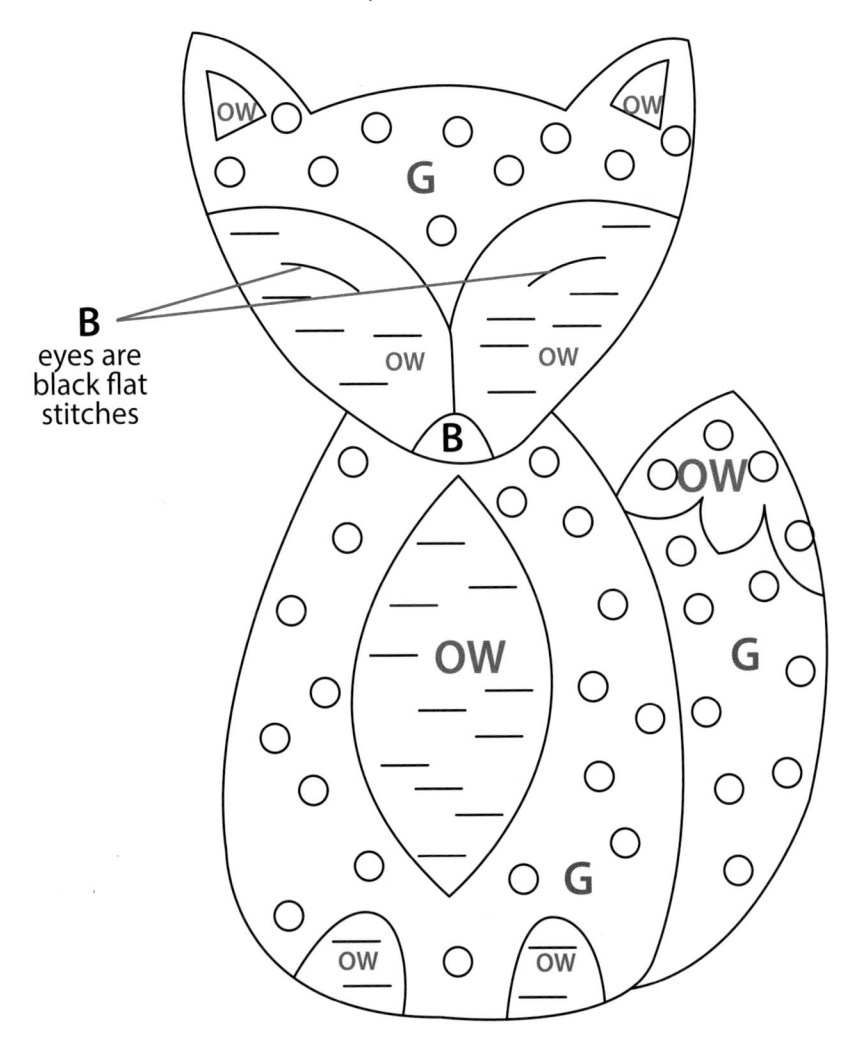

B
eyes are black flat stitches

Mermaid Pouch

― = Flat Stitch
○ = Loop Stitch
OW = Off-White
B = Blue
BG = Blue-Grey
MG = Metallic Gold

The Pouch pattern is full size.

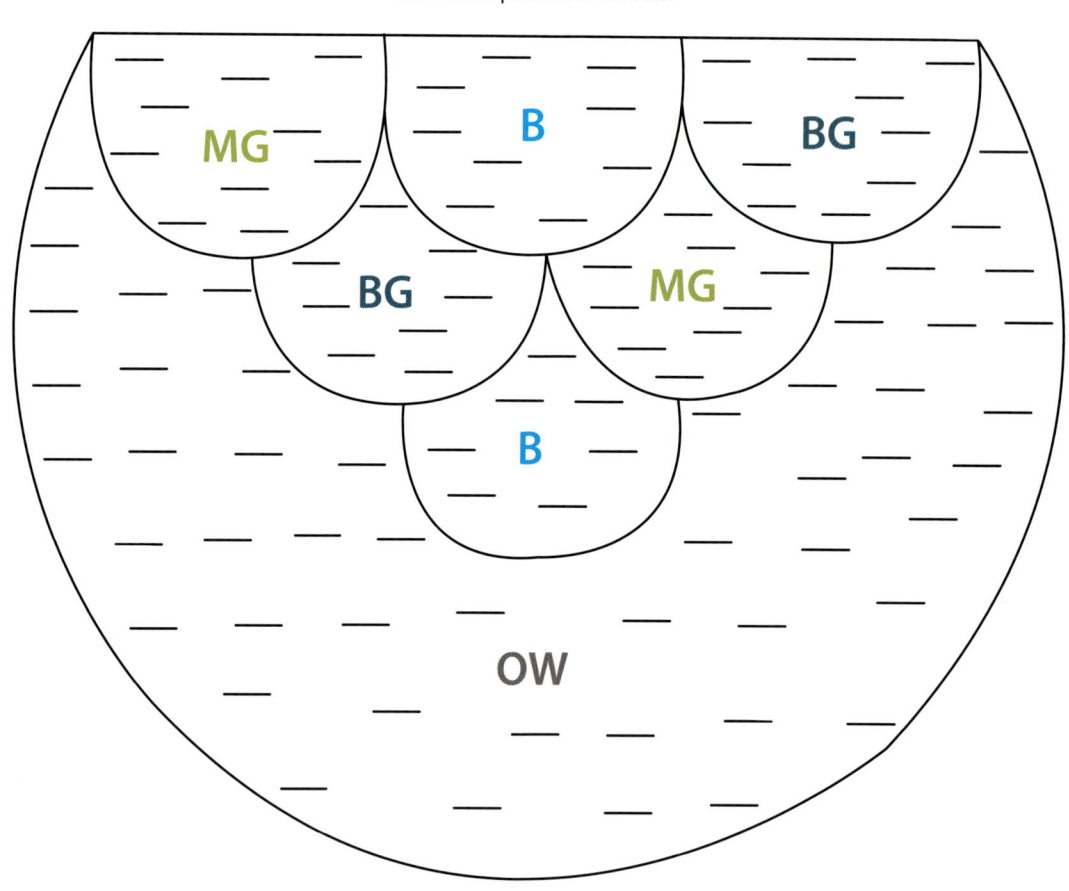

72 www.leisurearts.com

Pin Trio

◯ = Loop Stitch   M = Mustard   OW = Off-White   MC = Metallic Copper
P = Peach   T = Teal   DG = Dark Green   LR = Light Rose

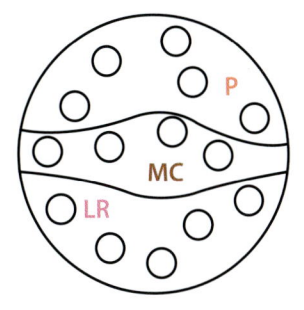

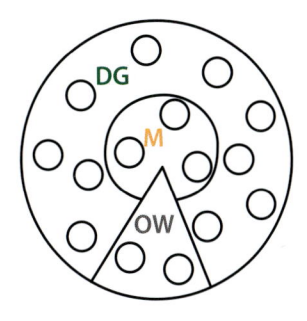

The Pin patterns are full size.

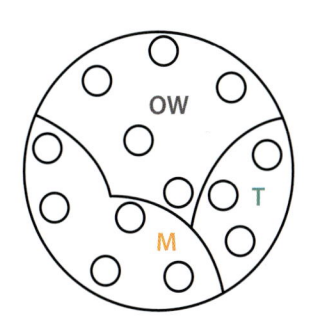

Storage Pouch

── = Flat Stitch
◯ = Loop Stitch
P = Peach
Y = Yellow
R = Rust
OW = Off-White

Photocopy Pouch pattern at 215%.

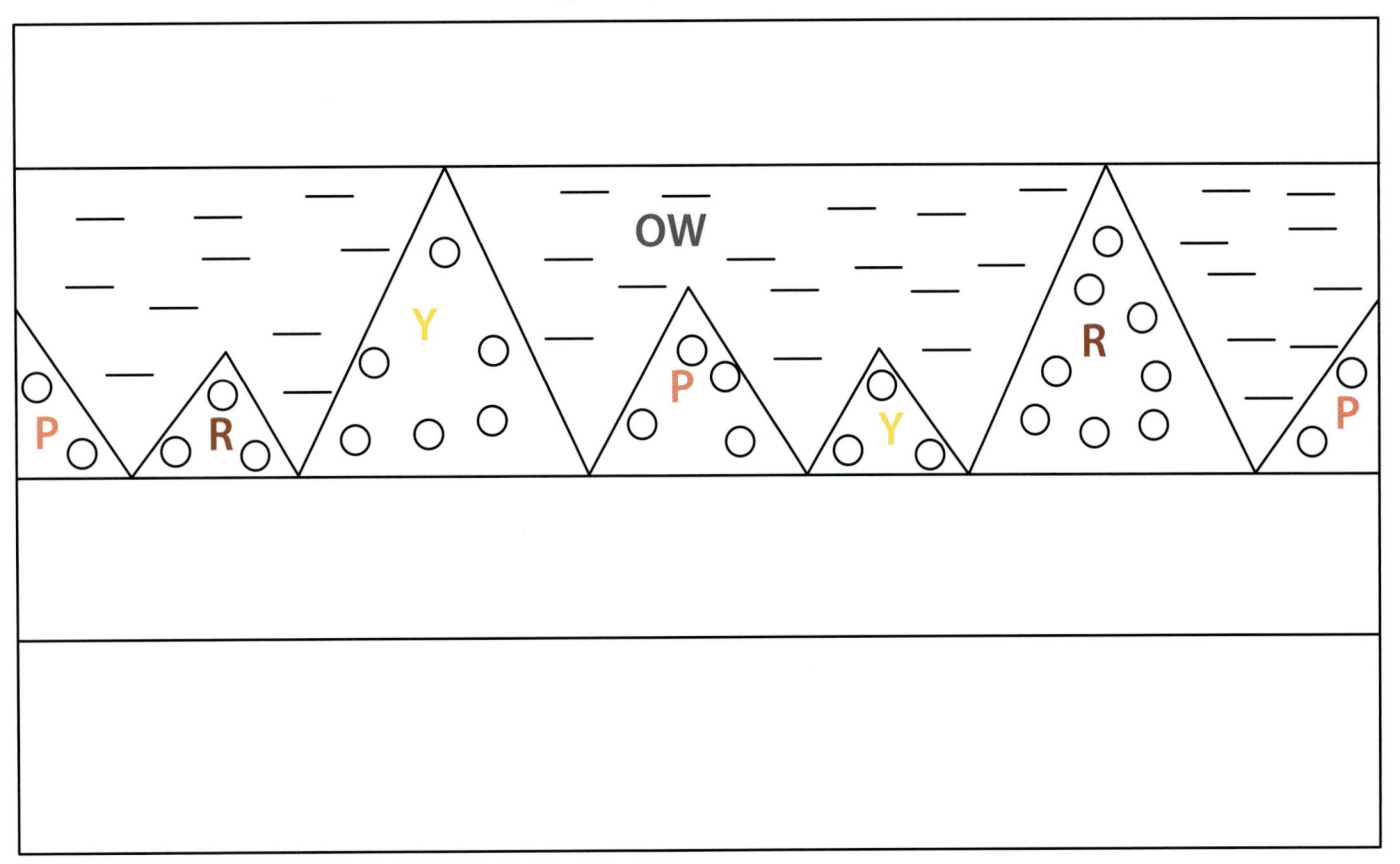

73

Floral Duo

— = Flat Stitch
○ = Loop Stitch
BK = Black
MC = Metallic Copper
C = Coral

The Floral patterns are full size.

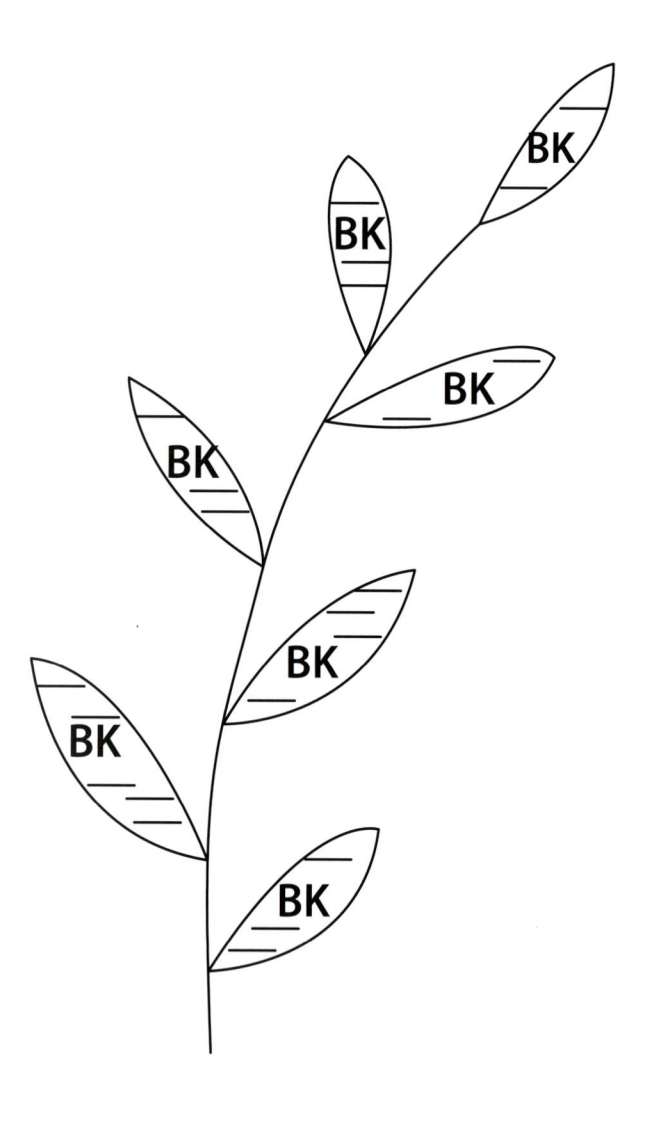

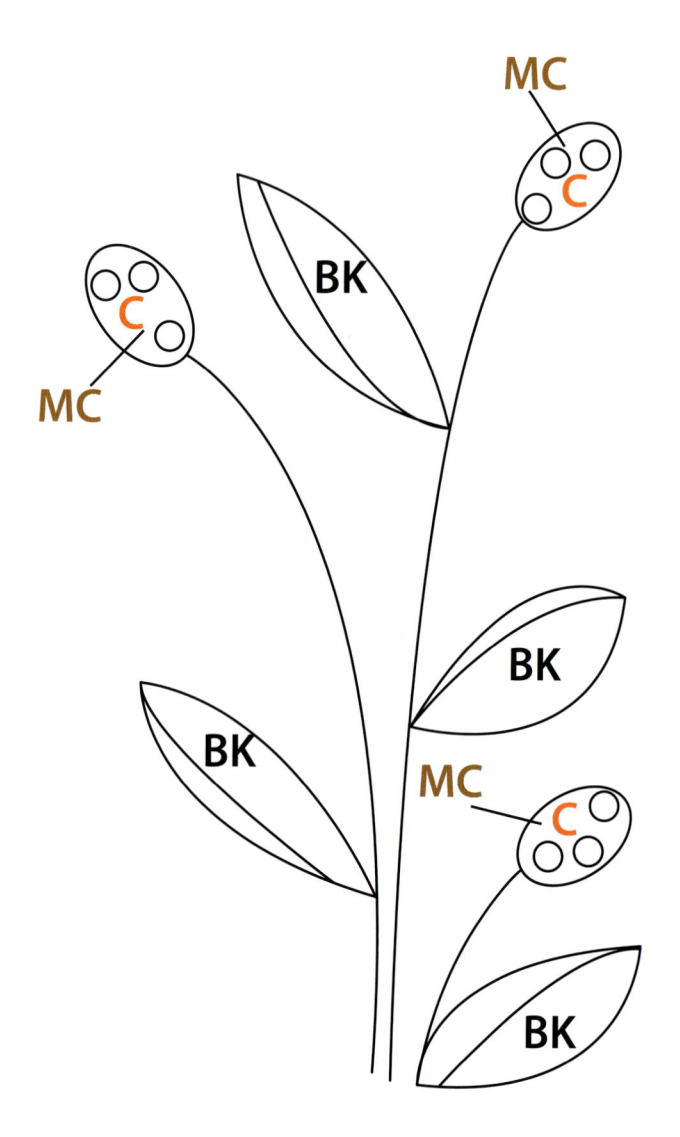

74   www.leisurearts.com

Denim Jacket

— = Flat Stitch
○ = Loop Stitch
BK = Black
R = Red
DR = Dark Red
G = Green
DG = Dark Green

The Jacket pattern is full size.

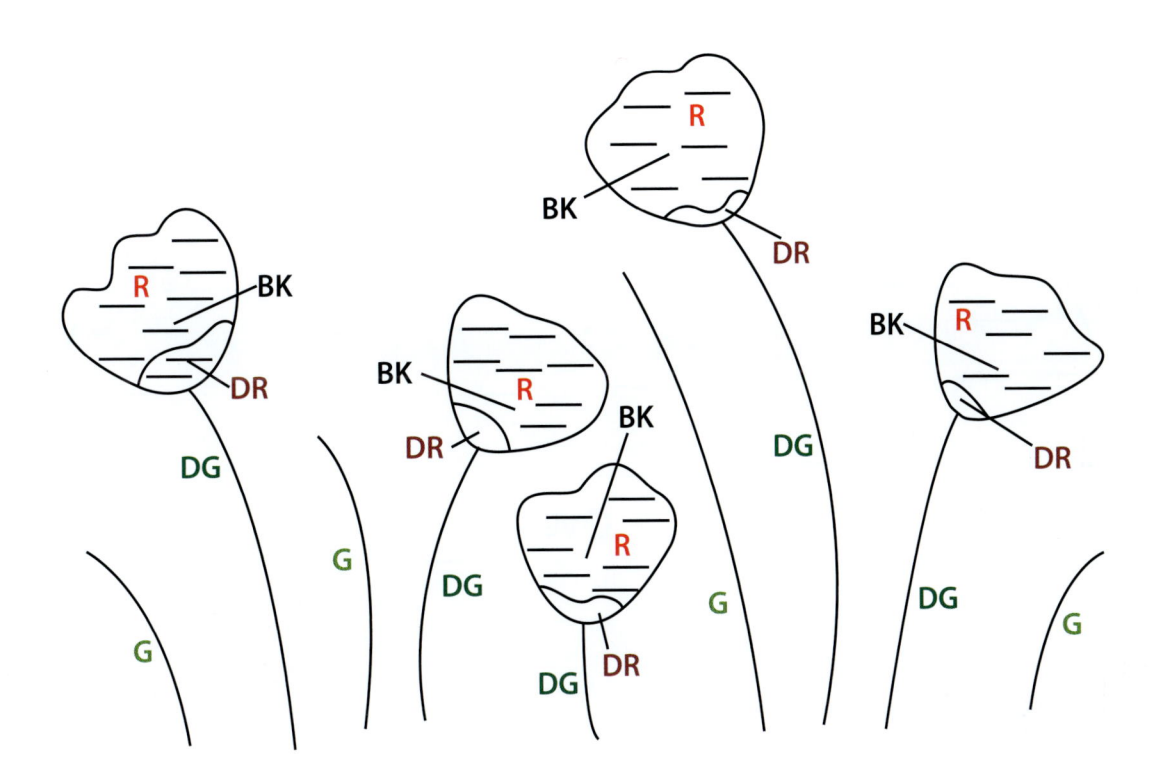

Purse

— = Flat Stitch
◯ = Loop Stitch
P = Peach
OW = Off-White
BG = Blue-Grey
T = Teal

Photocopy Purse pattern at 166%.

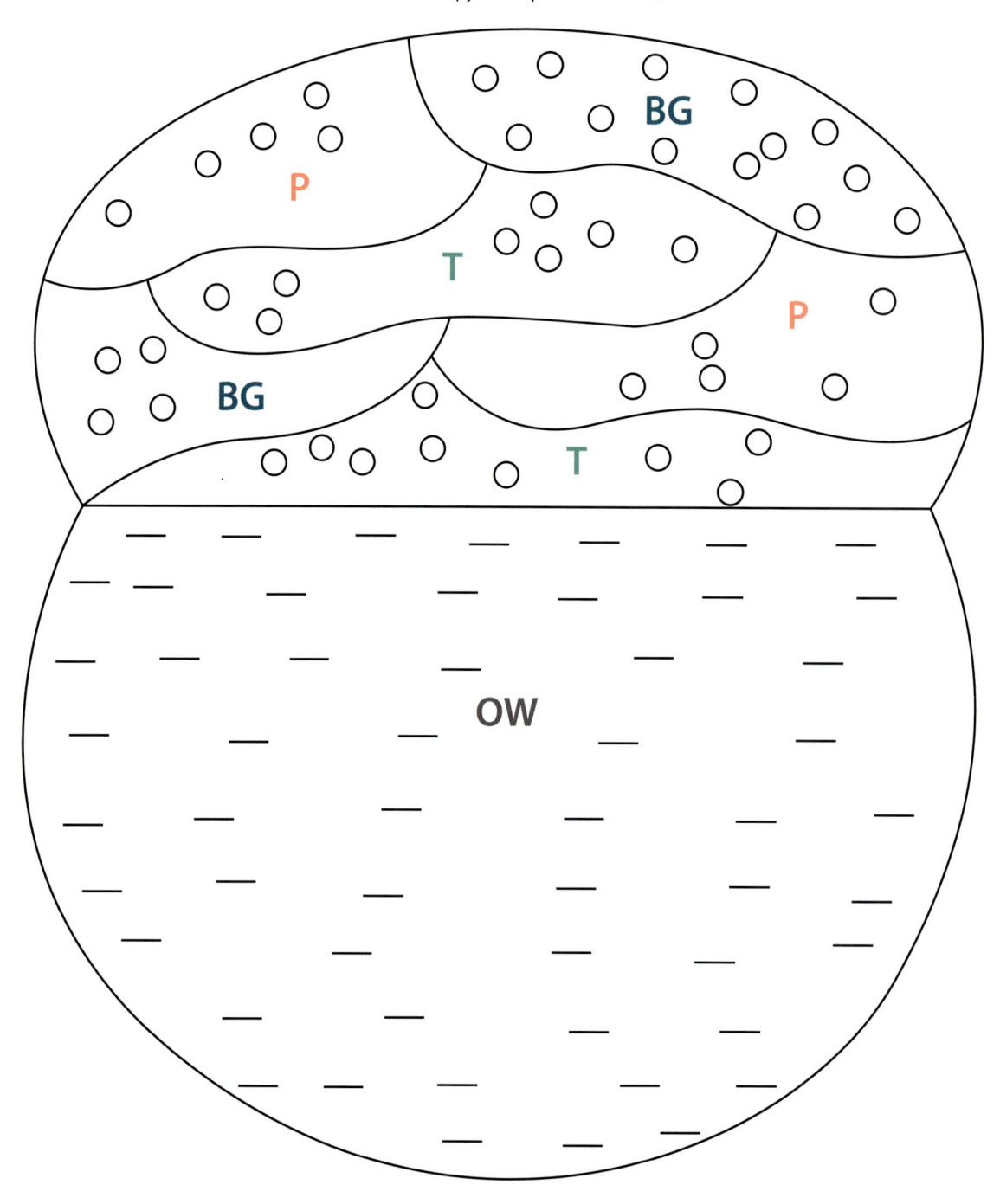

Penguin Toy

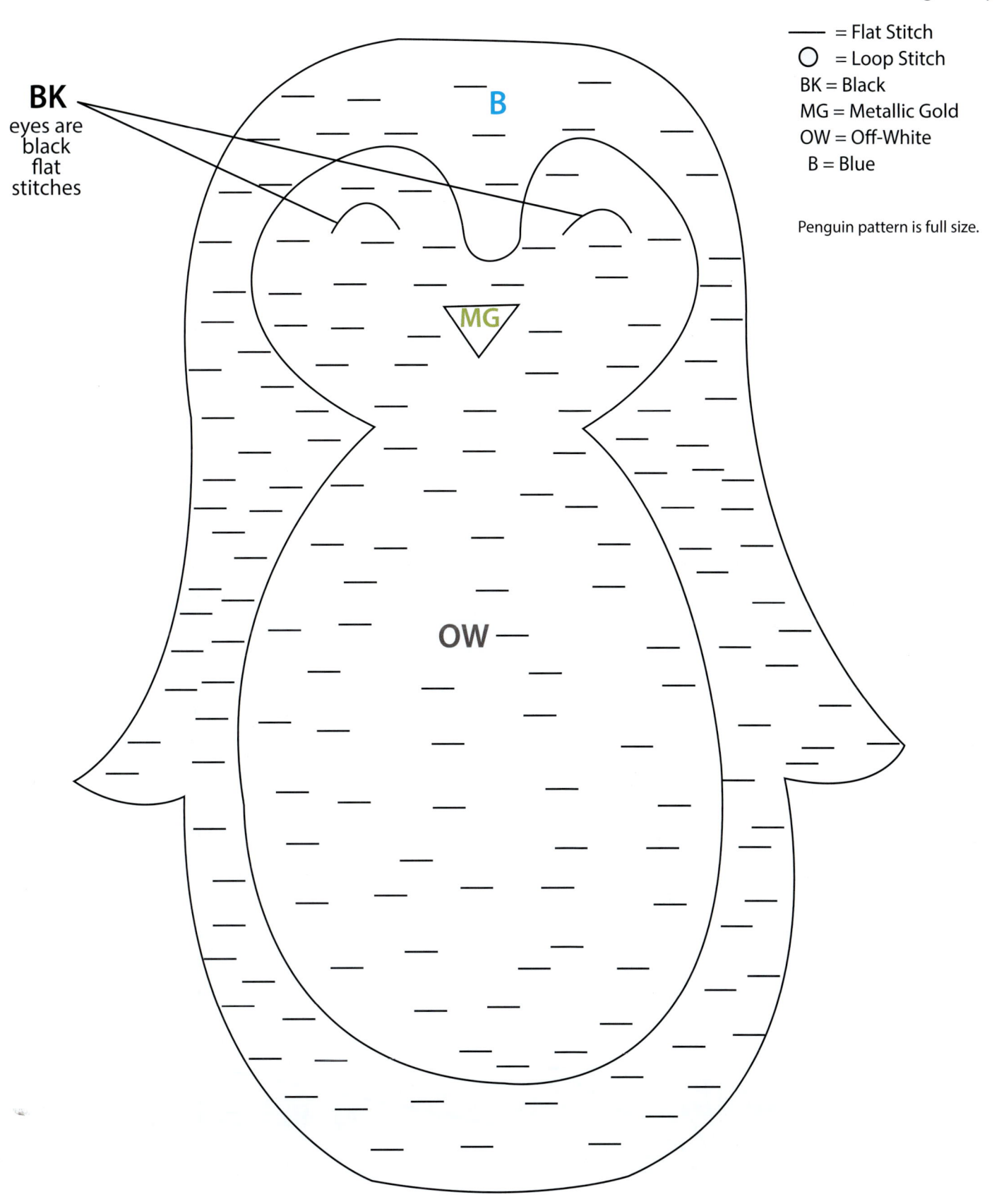

— = Flat Stitch
○ = Loop Stitch
BK = Black
MG = Metallic Gold
OW = Off-White
B = Blue

Penguin pattern is full size.

BK
eyes are black flat stitches

B

MG

OW

77

Coaster Set

◯ = Loop Stitch
P = Peach
R = Rust
E = Eggshell
MD = Mustard
PL = Plum
M = Mauve
A = Aqua

The Coaster patterns are full size.

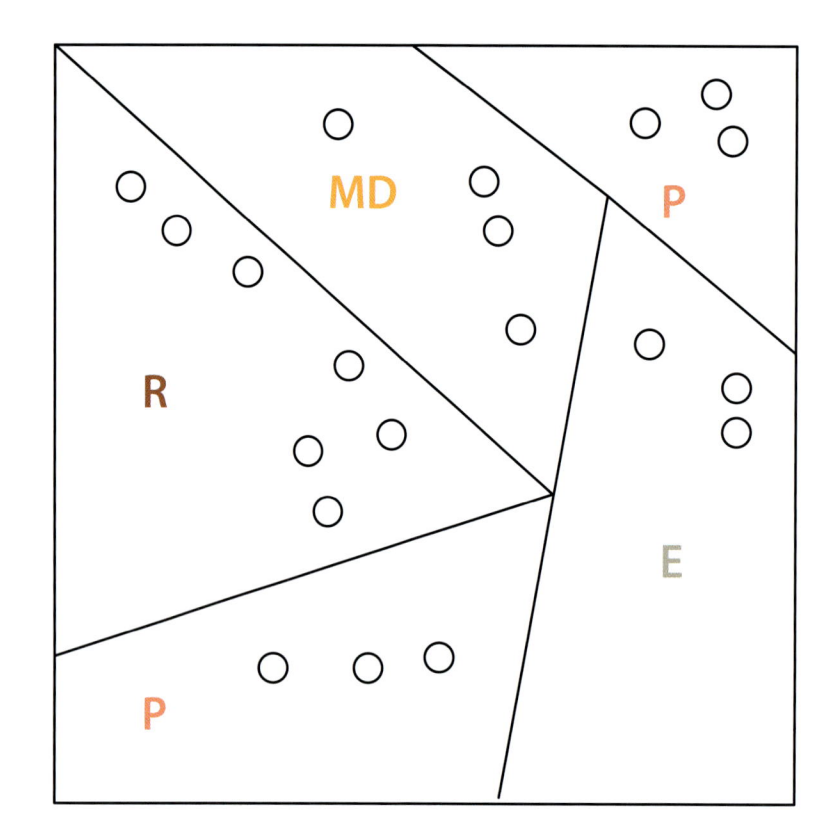

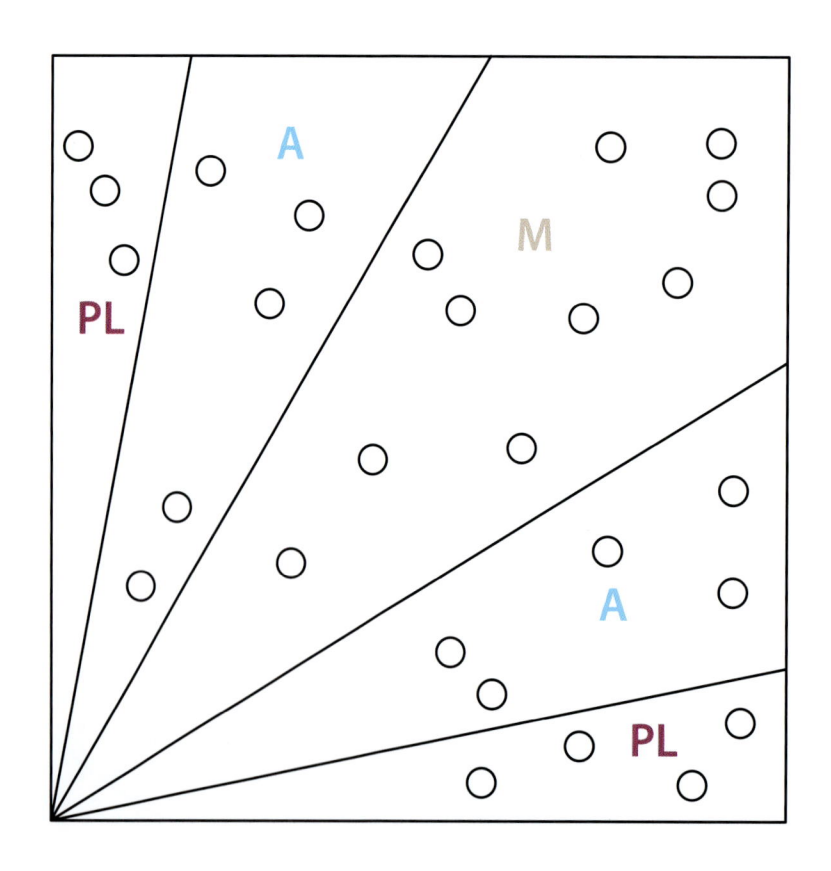

78   www.leisurearts.com

Rectangular Pillow

— = Flat Stitch   OW = Off-White   E = Eggshell
○ = Loop Stitch   P = Peach   CN = Cream/Navy Speckled
✕ = Shag Stitch   MD = Mustard   C = Coral
BG = Blue-Grey

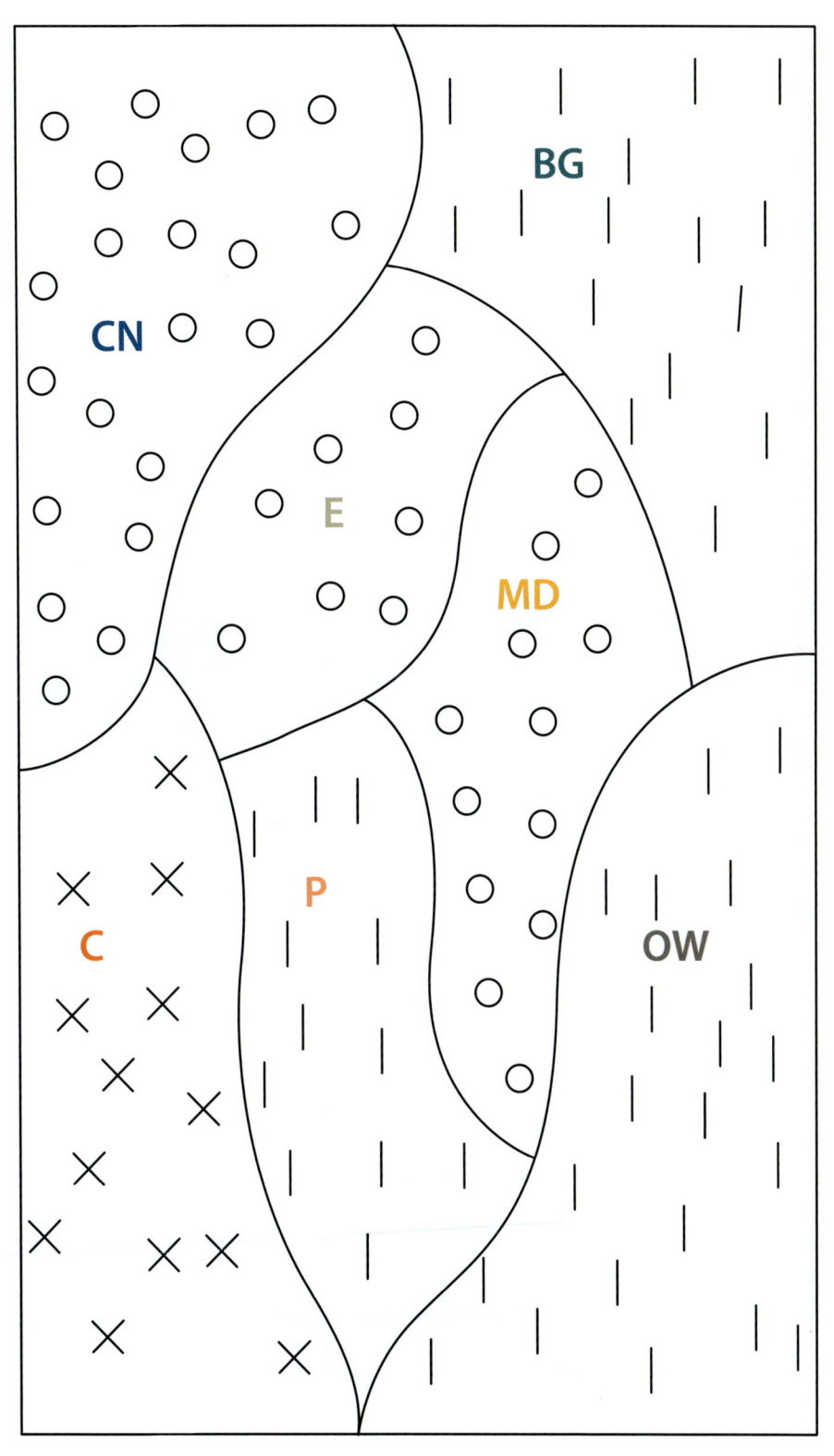

Photocopy Pillow pattern at 194%.

79

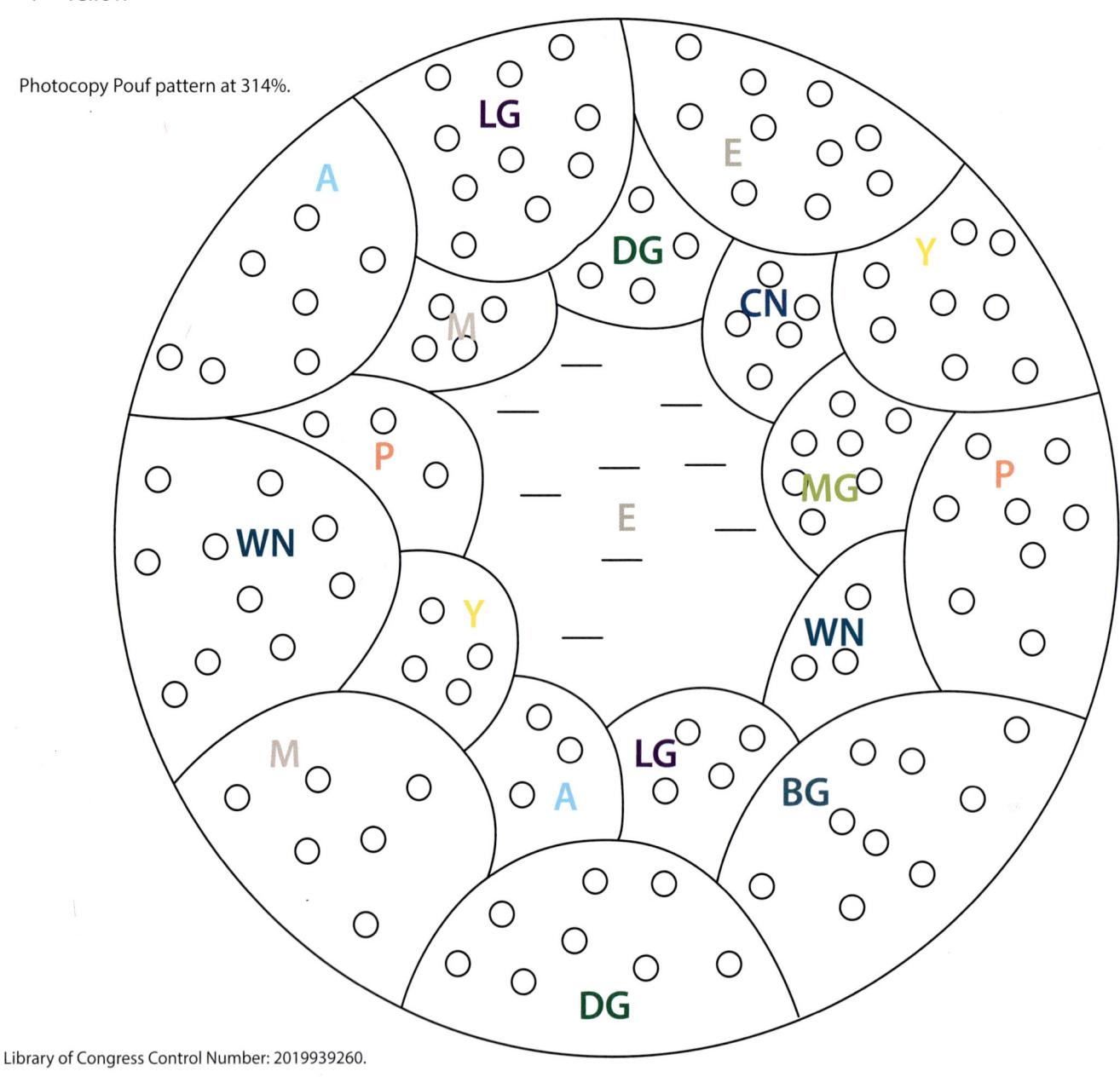

Round Pouf

- —— = Flat Stitch
- ◯ = Loop Stitch
- MG = Metallic Gold
- Y = Yellow
- P = Peach
- WN = White/Navy Speckled
- BG = Blue-Grey
- CN = Cream/Navy Speckled
- LG = Light Grey
- M = Mauve
- A = Aqua
- DG = Dark Green
- E = Eggshell

Photocopy Pouf pattern at 314%.

Library of Congress Control Number: 2019939260.

Made in U.S.A.

Copyright © 2019 by Leisure Arts, Inc., 104 Champs Blvd., STE 100, Maumelle, AR 72113-6738, www.leisurearts.com. All rights reserved. This publication is protected under federal copyright laws. Reproduction or distribution of this publication or any other Leisure Arts publication, including publications which are out of print, is prohibited unless specifically authorized. This includes, but is not limited to, any form of reproduction or distribution on or through the Internet, including posting, scanning, or e-mail transmission.

We have made every effort to ensure that these instructions are accurate and complete. We cannot, however, be responsible for human error, typographical mistakes, or variations in individual work.

Production Team: Technical Editor – Mary Sullivan Hutcheson; Technical Associate Editor – Lisa Lancaster; Senior Graphic Artist – Lora Puls; Graphic Artist – Kate Moul; Photo Stylist – Lori Wenger; Photographer – Jason Masters.

80 www.leisurearts.com